VODOU COSMOLOGY

VODOU COSMOLOGY
and the
HAITIAN REVOLUTION
in the Enlightenment Ideals of
KANT AND HEGEL

Vivaldi Jean-Marie

The University of the West Indies Press
Jamaica • Barbados • Trinidad and Tobago

The University of the West Indies Press
7A Gibraltar Hall Road, Mona
Kingston 7, Jamaica
www.uwipress.com

© 2018 Vivaldi Jean-Marie

All rights reserved. Published 2018

A catalogue record of this book is available from the National Library of Jamaica.

ISBN: 978-976-640-690-5 (print)
978-976-640-691-2 (Kindle)
978-976-640-692-9 (ePub)

Book design by Robert Harris
Cover image by Bianca Bonner-Harrison (Fleur d'Soleil)
Set in Minion 11/15 x 24
Printed in the United States of America

The University of the West Indies Press has no responsibility for the persistence or accuracy of URLs for external or third-party Internet websites referred to in this publication and does not guarantee that any content on such websites is, or will remain, accurate or appropriate.

For Devi, Clint and Marsha

Contents

    Introduction *1*

1. Vodou Cosmology, Haitian Subjectivity in Saint-Domingue and Hegel's Spirit *7*

2. Moral Autonomy in Vodou Cosmology and Kant's Ethics *25*

3. Hegel and Buck-Morss on the Misrecognition of Haitian Vodou's Contribution to the Haitian Revolution *42*

4. Vodou Cosmology as Methodology of the Haitian Revolution *57*

    Notes *73*
    Bibliography *79*
    Index *89*

Introduction

In the following four chapters, I set out to show that the inherent collective prowess of various African religious realities is responsible for the success of the Haitian Revolution. I use Vodou cosmology to mean the set of beliefs, rituals and norms which are inherent to various African religious realities as they were practised in Saint-Domingue and the ensuing collective attitudes that the adherents derive from these practices. Vodou cosmology emerged spontaneously out of the attempt to transcend the concomitant dissonance of displacement during slavery in Saint-Domingue and the adherents' quest to reproduce their original social and religious context. Also, given that the rise and unfolding of the transatlantic slave trade was concurrent with the rise of the Enlightenment and European empire, I thus provide my account of the elaboration of Vodou cosmology in Saint-Domingue in relation to the dominant ideals and practices of the Enlightenment. More specifically, I chose two canonical German philosophers of the Enlightenment, Immanuel Kant and G.W.F. Hegel, to show how their Enlightenment ideals methodically depicted Africans and people of African descent as "Negroes", to be both the inferior other of Europeans and the necessary raw materials for the wealth of the European empire. Furthermore, showing how Kant and Hegel's Enlightenment's ideals provide conceptual reinforcement for the transatlantic slave trade sheds light on the implicit and explicit participation of Enlightenment philosophers in creating and maintaining the institutions of the transatlantic slave trade.

The unifying thread of the chapters is that Vodou cosmology emerged in Saint-Domingue as both a mechanism of resistance to the reification of Africans and people of African descent and as a source of social, cultural, normative and spiritual practices for Africans and people of African descent to reclaim their humanity. As a mechanism of resistance and a technology for nation building, Vodou cosmology reached its zenith in the organization and occurrence of the Haitian Revolution, which challenged the conceptual role assigned to Africans and people of African descent in the Enlightenment ideals. Ultimately, the historical significance of Vodou cosmology is in the Haitian Revolution, which heralded the possibility of being of African descent and free. A frequent question that I had to address when presenting sections of this project to colleagues is: Why provide an account of Vodou and the Haitian Revolution in connection with the Enlightenment, more specifically the philosophies of Immanuel Kant and Hegel? My answer is that the problem that I set out to address is relatively new. Beside Susan Buck-Morss's *Hegel, Haiti, and Universal History* (2009), there is no other existing literature which contemplates the intricacies of Vodou practices, norms and beliefs from a philosophical angle. Accordingly, given that the problem of this project is new, I had to formulate the suitable terminologies since no adequate ready-made terminology is available.

The argument of the first chapter is that Vodou rituals and forced labour were conducive to the configuration of Haitian subjectivity in Saint-Domingue. I begin by showing that Haitian Vodou emerged out of the collective experience of its adherents and the syncretism of various African rituals. Collective experience stands for the unanticipated and systematic by-product of forced labour, which informs the adherents' social attitudes. Forced labour assumes the role of a formative process in enabling the slaves' assimilation in Saint-Domingue's social institutions via material production. Also, to situate Vodou cosmology and the configuration of Haitian subjectivity in Saint-Domingue within the larger context of the Enlightenment, I draw out some similarities between the adherents' experience with Hegel's central paradigm of the Lord and Bondsman in his *Phenomenology of Spirit* (1807), which is amenable to the account of forced labour which, I am arguing, shapes Haitian subjectivity. I borrow Hegel's paradigm because its currency contributes to the clarity of my argument about forced labour's role in enabling the slaves' assimilation in the social institutions of Saint-Domingue.

Building upon the previous chapter, chapter 2 argues that under Vodou cosmology, moral autonomy and validation are grounded in the community of Vodou adherents' reinforcement of moral judgements. Given that in Vodou cosmology, the collective is intrinsically tied to the individual, the moral autonomy of the individual thus depends on the collective reinforcement of the community of adherents. The issue of moral autonomy in Vodou cosmology is pertinent to the Enlightenment because it delineates how slave communities in Saint-Domingue define their moral autonomy vis-à-vis oppressive institutions in a similar fashion as the Enlightenment centred on assisting Westerners in overcoming the clergy's dogmatism throughout Europe. Chapter 2 shows that forced labour instilled the plural pronoun "we" as the marker of a pluralistic subjectivity among slave communities. My argument is that as an extension of this pluralistic subjectivity among slaves, moral autonomy is accordingly pluralistic instead of the individualistic model which is articulated in the moral autonomy of Westerners. On the basis of forced labour and Vodou cosmology, the practitioner asserts their moral autonomy via the collective.

To elaborate on my argument that moral autonomy and validation are grounded in the community of adherents' reinforcement of moral judgements, I draw out kinship between aspects of the adherent's ethical experience and some key concepts of the Enlightenment discourse about ethics presented in Kant's *Foundations of the Metaphysics of Morals* (1785) and *Critique of Practical Reason* (1788). In these texts, Kant grapples with similar aspects of the ethical experience of Westerners. Drawing an analogy between the Haitian Vodou adherent's ethical attitude and Kant's discourse about Westerners is pragmatic because it makes some unfamiliar aspects of the Vodou's adherent's ethical experience more comprehensible to readers who are not acquainted with the dynamics of Haitian Vodou. Also, it contributes to situating the discussion of subjectivity in Saint-Domingue within the larger context of the Enlightenment. The comparison aims to show that understanding the ethical experience, in the context of Vodou cosmology, requires a collective conceptualization of freedom in lieu of Kant's transcendental account of freedom as the starting point of ethical experience. On the basis of the comparison, I conclude that this collective account of freedom offers an alternative to Kant's analysis of moral autonomy and transcendental freedom.

The goal of chapter 3 is twofold. First, it argues that Hegel's omission of the significance of the Haitian Revolution in both the *Phenomenology of*

Spirit and the introduction to *The Philosophy of History* (1822, 1830–31) is deliberate and that this deliberate omission is the implication of his depiction of sub-Saharan African religious rituals through Protestant philosophical constructs in his *Philosophy of History*. Hegel's Protestant biased philosophical constructs against Africans and their religious reality blinded him to the inherent collective prowess of their religious reality, which made the Haitian Revolution possible. These Protestant philosophical biases and his hostility toward Africans' religious reality lead Hegel to depict the rich and complex religious practices of sub-Saharan Africans as mere chaos and idolatry. Hegel relies on this depiction to fashion Africans as "Negroes" – Godless, barbaric, cruel and whose disposition makes enslavement their natural merit. It is in virtue of this carefully crafted strategy to delineate Africans as barbaric and the inferior other of Europeans that Hegel provides a conceptual means to the transatlantic slave trade. Ultimately, under Hegel's philosophical pen, Africans and people of African descent are classed as a people whose main contribution to Western culture was slavery or to have availed themselves as mere tools of wealth production.

The argument of the last chapter is that Vodou cosmology granted the slave communities of Saint-Domingue the religious unity, language and achievement of a common destiny as the requisites of state formation and the conviction of universal humanity that made the Haitian Revolution a successful critique and expansion of the Enlightenment's ideals. To make this argument, I show that overcoming tribal differences and the intersection of Vodou practices and marronage in Saint-Domingue contributed to the elaboration of a shared national identity. I borrow Neil Roberts's paradigm, which states:

> Marronage (marronage, maroonage, maronage) conventionally refers to a group of persons isolating themselves from a surrounding society in order to create a fully autonomous community, and for centuries it has been integral to interpreting the idea of freedom in Haiti as well as other Caribbean islands and Latin American countries including the Dominican Republic, Jamaica, Suriname, Venezuela, Brazil, Cuba, Colombia, and Mexico. These communities of freedom – known variously as "maroon societies", *quilombos, palenques, mocambos, cumbes, mambises, Rancherias, ladeiras, magotes, and manieles* – geographically situate themselves from areas slightly outside the

borders of a plantation to the highest mountains of a region located as a far away from plantation life as possible.[1]

Also, given that I am arguing that the Haitian Revolution was a critique of the Enlightenment ideals of freedom and that it expands the prevailing Enlightenment view of freedom by extending it to the slaves of Saint-Domingue, I provide a discussion of Kant's essay *What Is Enlightenment?* (1784) as well as his outlook on slavery and African peoples as colonial commodities in *The Science of Right* (1790) to show that Kant's ideals of the Enlightenment were European male–centred and presupposed freedom from forced labour to be fulfilled. These ideals assert European humanity in contradistinction to slaves as colonial commodities. To further the critique of the Enlightenment's ideals, I engage with Michel Rolph-Trouillot's critique of the Enlightenment to prove that his view that the Haitian Revolution was unthinkable from the perspective of the leaders and slaves of Saint-Domingue is the implication of his implicit espousal of the Enlightenment's depiction of African slaves. It concludes that religious unity, language and the achievement of a common destiny, which derive from Vodou cosmology, made the Haitian Revolution a cohesive and strategic historical event.

I conclude that the Haitian Revolution heralded the African Diaspora Enlightenment because it granted the slaves the consciousness of being of African descent and free, an idea that was anathema to the purview of Eurocentric ideals. It created the occasion for the slaves to overcome both physical and rational subjugation. The tyranny of the monarchy and organized religion that Kant repudiates is the equivalent of the colonialist regime and the justification of slavery by the edicts of *Le Code Noir* in the French colonies. Through the occurrence of the Haitian Revolution, people of African descent became free social agents and the centre of their sociopolitical context. Furthermore, the occurrence of the Haitian Revolution undertakes a paradoxical shift of the Enlightenment. It displaces its conceptual purview in showing that reason, the central lynchpin of the Enlightenment, prevailed in slave communities. It allows the slaves to secure the recognition of the West, as both humans and *res cogitans* – entities that are fit to reason and behave as sociopolitical agents. This recognition is articulated in the emergence of Saint-Domingue as the Republic of Haiti, the first black nation.

Thus, the news of the Haitian Revolution was subversive among other slave communities because it triggered the consciousness of the possibility of being of African descent and free, which is synthesized in blackness, black power and black cultural expressions.

CHAPTER 1.

Vodou Cosmology, Haitian Subjectivity in Saint-Domingue and Hegel's Spirit

The argument of this chapter is that Vodou rituals and forced labour were conducive to the configuration of Haitian subjectivity in Saint-Domingue. To make this argument, I begin by showing that Haitian Vodou emerged out of the collective experience of its adherents and the syncretism of various African rituals. Collective experience stands for the unanticipated and systematic by-product of forced labour, which informs the adherents' social attitudes. Forced labour assumes the role of a formative process in enabling the slaves' assimilation in Saint-Domingue's social institutions via material production. Also, to situate Vodou cosmology and the configuration of Haitian subjectivity in Saint-Domingue within the larger context of the Enlightenment, I draw out some similarities between the adherents' experience with Hegel's central paradigm of the Lord and Bondsman in his *Phenomenology of Spirit*, which is amenable to the account on forced labour which, I am arguing, shapes Haitian subjectivity. I borrow Hegel's paradigm because its currency contributes to the clarity of my argument about forced labour's role in enabling the slaves' assimilation in the social institutions of Saint-Domingue.

Vodou cosmology stands for the set of beliefs, rituals and norms which are inherent to various African religious realities as they were practised in Saint-Domingue and the ensuing collective attitudes that the adherents derive from these practices. It emerged spontaneously out of the attempt to transcend the concomitant dissonance of displacement during slavery in Saint-Domingue and the adherents' quest to create their original social and religious context. While discussion of the spiritual dimension of Haitian Vodou is widespread, the elaboration of its cosmology is sensitive to the import of the rituals in the social experience of adherents as social agents – more specifically, how the adherents' social agency is informed by the Vodou rituals. This secular consideration expands the dominant religious and spiritual interpretation of Haitian Vodou in elaborating its social implications.

The literature about Haitian Vodou unfolds along two axes. One tradition, whose main proponent, Justin Dorsainvil, in his *Vodou et Névrose* (1913), considers Vodou as the outlet for collective neurosis through religious practices. The other tradition espouses an apologetic account of Vodou. The apologetic take on Vodou, which is espoused by the Négritude movement, casts Haitian Vodou as a distinct Caribbean cultural expression and spirituality. In particular, this outlook found a voice among Haitian intellectuals who presented Vodou as a common African heritage shared by both mulattos and dark-skinned Haitians in an effort to improve social class relations. One famous proponent of such approach is the Haitian sociologist Jean Price-Mars's classic text *Ainsi Parla l'Oncle* (1928). Price-Mars launched a vibrant movement for the defence of Vodou as central to Haitian folklore. Furthermore, the regional shift in attitudes toward national folklore in Latin America struck a responsive chord among certain sectors of the Haitian elite, who claimed newfound pride in their African ancestry.[1]

However, the shortcoming of the apologetic account is that it overlooks the role of Vodou practices in informing the social experience of its practitioners. In striving to secure favourable reception of Vodou by the Haitian elite and the West, it merely emphasizes the aesthetics of the rituals and neglects their import to the adherents' social attitudes. Also, Price-Mars's exposition downplays the African heritage of Haitian Vodou and depicts it as a unique form of Haitian cultural expression. Elaborating the latent social aspect of Haitian Vodou transcends the standard spiritual and cultural accounts to draw out how the practitioners derive some of their social and ethical guidelines from the rituals and beliefs. Accordingly, the guiding assumption is that in Saint-Domingue, Haitian Vodou emerged as a set of collective and spiritual practices which bear significant social and normative implications.

Forced Labour and the Rise of Vodou Cosmology

A close examination of Haitian Vodou's provenance reveals its root in slaves' ancestral rituals. These rituals are important because they provide a communal technology to displaced slaves to align themselves with their ancestral lineage. These rituals preserve the tribal identity of the adherents and grant them the requisite resources to function socially in Saint-Domingue. The social aspect of these religious rituals consists in the adherent's preservation of their previous social self-conceptualization. By means of the rituals, the adherents reclaim how they conceptualize themselves in their original African context. The ancestral rituals thus illustrate the adherents' collective attempt to resist the dissonance and alienation inherent to slavery. Maya Deren is sensitive to the social prowess of Haitian Vodou in observing that "Voudoun was a collective creation, it did not exact the abandonment of one tribal deity in favour of another. On the contrary, it seemed rather to delight in as generous an inclusion as possible."[2] Vodou rituals refigure both the spiritual purpose of different tribal deities and the social roles and injunctions that they impose upon the adherents.

This religious syncretism shapes the social and ethical attitudes of the adherents. To make my argument, I am using the paradigm of syncretism, which holds that "as the study of acculturation, contact between carriers of different cultures. . . . Each culture, with its economic, political, religious, kinship and other institutions, was further conceptualized as being composed of smaller parts called culture traits which combined to form patterns and complexes. Like whole cultures, cultural traits, patterns and complexes, along with the institutions they formed, were believed to have their own specific histories."[3]

This paradigm is suitable because the slaves who were shipped to Saint-Domingue came from distinct African cultures with specific cultural traits, patterns and complexes. Accordingly, Vodou cosmology is the unanticipated spiritual and social formation which emerged from Saint-Domingue's slave communities attempting to bridge their different cultures in a meaningful fashion. Vodou cosmology is the social synthesis which results from the complex brokering process of the various cultural, religious, economic and political inheritance of each group of slaves. Internalization of this social synthesis created a distinctive form of subjectivity. This form of subjectivity, which is endemic to Saint-Domingue, is born out of the import of this religious, social and cultural syncretism of the Vodou practitioners. The subjective reality of the adherents becomes heterogeneous in virtue of such syncretism. As Lilas Desquiron observes: "Le culte des ancêtres est le point de rencontre privilégié entre le social et le sacré, entre le séculier et le religieux."[4] (The ancestors' ritual is the privileged intersection between the social and the sacred, between the secular and the religious.) Displacement impaired the rituals which were central to slaves' pre-existing religious identities and compelled the practitioners to rely on religious and social memory to reproduce them in Saint-Domingue. Reproducing the rituals created continuity between the social institutions of the previous tribal context with the slaves' social reality in Saint-Domingue. By engaging in the rituals, the adherents kindle sociocultural memory to overcome the rupture of social identity which results from slavery. It is noteworthy that the process of pairing various religious rituals and norms elaborated an unprecedented religious and social reality, which is informed by previous African religious realities, while having a distinctive geographical and heterogeneous context.

The attempts of slaves from different tribes to reproduce ancestral rituals constitute the first syncretism of Vodou. Each society maintained its own ancestral traditions, and through interactions with one another they modified their beliefs and practices to meet their new situation.[5] Religious negotiations among members of different tribes were the initial step toward this collective attitude. Brokering the ancestral traditions leads to the transcendence of religious and social homogeneity; it elaborates a socio-epistemic space for different tribal practitioners in the subjective reality of the adherents. Each adherent learned to validate the rituals of her neighbour while simultaneously acknowledging her as a social neighbour. The second form of syncretism consists of the heterogeneous disposition that it instils in adherents. Each adherent transcends the homogeneity of her original set of rituals and assimilates the neighbour's rituals. This process makes the adherent's subjectivity heterogeneous. The religious, social and epistemic aspects of this process delineate the collective attitude inherent to Vodou cosmology.

On the other hand, Vodou encapsulates the failure to reproduce the ancestral rituals in toto. Vodou provides a substitute for the ancestral rituals which traditionally occurred in the intimate context of the adherents' family. In Saint-Domingue, Vodou was thus a remedial alternative to restore the family structure, which was dismantled by slavery. Vodou practices were public and collectively organized in Saint-Domingue to create familial bonds among isolated slaves. The public rituals of the hounfor (Vodou temple) are, in a sense, an extension of the principles which govern a family, where the cooperative participation of all the members – including the children – is necessary for survival.[6] Vodou practices mend the familial gap created by the absence of relatives in transforming the adherents into an extended network of significant others. Accordingly, through the rituals, each adherent becomes a religious relative and social neighbour. Moreover, Haitian Vodou fulfils the adherents' yearning for their tribal lifestyle. It synthesizes the psychological and social needs of the adherents in a collective reality. The organization of the hounfor and the objects contained in the bagi (altar room) confirm and elaborate the civil organization of Vodoun. When there is no ceremony going on, all kinds of daily activities take place throughout the court and peristyle (Vodou shrine). Although every hounfor varies, depending on region, wealth or local custom, the space always allows the cooperative participation of all members.[7] Even though the layout of the hounfor varies from one region to another according to the slave communities that lived there during slavery, every hounfor is congenial to civil cooperation among the members of the given village. Vodou provided these communities with the technology to guide social and religious assimilation in Saint-Domingue while also affirming their distinctiveness. It was the focus for the development of political consciousness so far as it allowed the slaves to be aware that their values were different from those of the whites and also as far as it allowed them to express their negritude.[8]

Establishing a common religious and social identity makes Vodou cosmology collective. The slaves retained elements of the culture which they had known in Africa, and in particular the Vodou religion, which was widely practised on the plantations. It was an amalgam of the various religious beliefs and practices of West Africa, which even incorporated certain Christian symbols.[9] Nicholls's observation captures the syncretistic essence of Vodou practices in accommodating Christian symbols. It is proof of the collective nature of Vodou which imbibes non-African religious practices as well. The inherent syncretism of Vodou sheds light on the dual religious identity of Vodou practitioners who are at ease in summoning both Catholic saints and Vodou deities. For example, a typical Vodou ceremony unfolds as follows:

> First would come the salutations and the parade of the flags. Signs of respect are shown among the dignitaries, for example, the "hounsis" (Voodoo initiates) turning three times in front of the "houngan" (Voodoo priest), and kissing the ground, or the dignitaries kissing the flags. Then would come the invocations to the god and ancestors being honoured, beginning often with *"in the name of the Father, and of the Son, and of the Holy spirit"*. The invocations are followed by the libations or special salutations with water, in front of the sacred objects, and the spiritual drawing of the "vévés" (symbolic signs of the gods) on the floor of the peristyle with powder or flour, accompanied with sacred prayers and ceremonial gestures.[10]

Syncretism and the methodical organization of the rituals illustrate the collective and social aspects of Haitian Vodou. The traditional religions of Africa could hardly be perpetuated in toto in the New World because of the vast ecological differences between the continents.[11] Vodou practitioners faced the challenge of creating rituals which suit the context of Saint-Domingue while also being consistent with African rituals. Thus, they had to depend on cultural memory and imagination to overcome these ecological differences. Establishing continuity between the institutions of their previous African context with those of Saint-Domingue is at the core of Vodou cosmology. Despite geographical and tribal differences, the displaced slaves in the Catholic regime managed to invent the suitable practices to preserve their African inheritance. Neo-African cults, found in countries which are predominantly Catholic, have incorporated a considerable body of African traditions in their beliefs and rituals.[12] The rise of Vodou cosmology is the outcome of a collective process to derive a common ethos and social compass. This social dimension is inherent to the rituals and articulates the dual function of Haitian Vodou in Saint-Domingue as being both social and spiritual. For Desquiron, Vodou practices perform a "dual syncretism": "Le Vodou haïtien est le produit d'un double syncrétisme: le premier s'est accompli entre les différentes cultures africaines; le deuxième a eu lieu entre ces différentes cultures africaines et la culture occidentale."[13] (Haitian Vodou is the product of a dual syncretism: the first happened among the different African cultures;

the second happened between these different African cultures and Western culture.) Desquiron's observation denies the prevalent assumption that slave communities were monolithic and freed of social challenges.

The development of Haitian Vodou was concurrent with the slaves' elaboration of both the appropriate practices and a socio-ethical map to create cohesive social communities. In this deeply alienating context, religion certainly provided an institution through which the African past of the slaves was perpetuated and also an instrument of solidarity and communication during the colonial period.[14] Vodou practices provide the media for solidarity and effective communication among adherents. One of the major challenges that Haitian Vodou had to overcome was the legal and religious restraints of *Le Code Noir* – a series of restrictions on the practice of any religion other than Roman Catholicism in the French colonies. During its early phase, the practitioners had to mediate the rituals with these restrictions. This mediation contributed to the syncretistic nature of Vodou and made it a secretive religion. It is noteworthy that this outdated restriction by *Le Code Noir* is responsible for the secretive occurrences of the rituals and the stigmas associated with Haitian Vodou. Haitian Vodou, in reality, is a harmless mixture of religious beliefs of African origin, with the Christian or, more exactly, the Catholic faith. As a religion, it aims at honouring its gods and spiritual entities.[15] The adherents managed to overcome the colonial mandate of *Le Code Noir* to salvage the integrity of the rituals, which thrived as creolized religious practices. Thus, Vodou has to be characterized as a generic term, covering these various creolized cults.[16] The subjective reality of the practitioners absorbed these creolized rituals as well. Creolization consists of the meditation of colonial institutions with the African legacy of the slave communities of Saint-Domingue. It is one form of the social expressions of Vodou cosmology.

One implication of the process of overcoming tribal differences and creating a common identity is that it compels the adherent's subjectivity to abide by the plural pronoun "we" as the marker of the collective, instead of the singular pronoun "I" as the classic marker of Western subjectivity. Adopting "we" as the marker of their subjectivity was a logical by-product of syncretism and the collective process of Vodou cosmology. It is proof of the mediation that occurs in the rituals and social institutions of Saint-Domingue. Vodou was perhaps one of the most cohesive forces among the slaves and one which the whites tried to suppress.[17] Vodou practices were threatening toward the colonial institutions of Saint-Domingue. The colonial establishment was cognizant of the social prowess of Vodou practices as an alternative source of social norms for slave communities.

Vodou Cosmology and Collective Identity

Social bonding in the rituals provided the arena for the worshippers to acknowledge each other as a constituent of one's individual identity. The social neighbour is included in one's structural reference of meaning via collective participation in the rituals. After all, taking part in the activities of a cult or sect provides emotional support for members who are forced to live in a world that they often perceive as hostile, thereby allowing for the possibility of collective action.[18] Vodou rituals granted the slaves a sense of common social destiny and confidence in a potential national identity despite the legal and religious restrictions of *Le Code Noir*. Indeed, the edicts of *Le Code Noir* were aimed at hindering social unity among slaves. The rituals performed the spiritual and social reversal of *Le Code Noir*'s agenda, which aimed at reinforcing the isolated plantation mentality among the slaves under religious prohibition. The task of reconciliation among the slaves shipped to Saint-Domingue, hardly an issue of redistributing wealth, concerned building fraternal alliances of trust among former enemies of war and among persons massed together in labour gangs who had no common background and little understanding of each other – indeed, they may not have known of each other's cultural existence before the crossing.[19] Overcoming tribal differences, trust-building and social alliances via Vodou rituals laid the foundation of slave communities as a distinctive society in Saint-Domingue.

Furthermore, the social impulse of the rituals is plain in their judicious organization. Each adherent assumes a specific role. Even though the primary purpose is spiritual, the methodical performance of each participant in the event defines her dual function as a spiritual and social fellow. Marie-José Alcide thinks that "stage directing may also be observed in the organization of the ceremonies. The celebration is the product of teamwork. The roles are carefully distributed, and each member bears special responsibilities."[20] The organization of the rituals illustrates the continuity between spirituality and collective socialization in Vodou cosmology. Thus, the rituals provide the basis of social recognition and agency in virtue of the assigned role that adherents assume. In the observation below, Dubois depicts the lakou – a courtyard where rituals occur – as the arena in which spirituality and socialization intersect in Vodou cosmology:

> In its most basic sense, a lakou (from the French la cour, or courtyard) refers to a group of houses – sometimes including a dozen or more structures, and usually owned by an extended family – gathered around a common yard. But the lakou also came to represent specific social conventions meant to guarantee each person equal access to dignity and individual freedom. Religious life, too, served to hold this world together. Each lakou included a set of family tombs, allowing residents of the countryside to do something that had been difficult if not impossible under slavery itself: to keep and maintain a cemetery, paying respects to the dead and through them honoring more distant ancestors in Africa.[21]

The *lakou* system is in tune with the adherents' search for validation from ancestors, departed spirits and contemporary participants. In fulfilling this need, the rituals that take place in the *lakou* are conducive to meaningful social interaction in providing the platform for the development of social agency. The configuration of the rituals unfolds concurrently with Vodou cosmology around a common purpose, namely the attempt to elaborate a meaningful social context for the adherents which resembles their previous African reality. Elaborating a meaningful social context via the rituals prompted a collective appropriation of Saint-Domingue by the slaves. The configuration of the rituals and Vodou cosmology prompted an unanticipated form of consciousness – in other words, the slave became conscious of herself as an essential constituent of Saint-Domingue's sociopolitical affairs. The rise of this form of consciousness assisted the slaves in transcending their outlook on Saint-Domingue as a foreign land. Saint-Domingue gradually became home as the rituals reinforced the slaves' consciousness of their social agency.

Another pivotal contribution of Vodou cosmology is that it eased the adherents' assimilation in Saint-Domingue's institutions. It provided the spiritual and social technology to appropriate the geographical and sociopolitical setting of Saint-Domingue. Vodou cosmology produced a dual identity: the slave started to self-conceptualize as being an African and Saint-Dominguois. The consciousness of citizenship and the appropriation of the material context of Saint-Domingue unfolded simultaneously with the slaves' ability to mould their geographical environment. The dynamics and nuances of imposing Vodou cosmology upon the material context of Saint-Domingue through forced labour is illustrated in what Hegel refers to as the "formative activity" in his discussion of the Lord and Bondsman:

> This negative middle term or the formative activity is at the same time the individuality or pure being-for-self of consciousness which now, in the work outside of it, acquires an element of permanence. It is in this way, therefore, that consciousness, qua worker, comes to see in the independent being [of the object] its own independence.... Through this discovery of himself by himself, the bondsman realizes that it is precisely in his work wherein he seemed to have only an alienated existence that he acquires a mind of his own.[22]

Hegel's account of labour as a formative activity and a medium for the elaboration of self-consciousness in the slave is pertinent to the discussion of Vodou cosmology and slavery in Saint-Domingue. It situates Vodou cosmology and the formation of a distinctive subjectivity in Saint-Domingue within the larger context of the Enlightenment. The slave communities of Saint-Domingue fulfilled Hegel's paradigm above because it is through forced labour on the plantations that they overcame their alienation in Saint-Domingue; they ceased to view themselves as mere slaves in viewing the products of their labour as concrete realizations of their self-consciousness on Saint-Domingue's soil. The rise of self-consciousness that Hegel assigns to the Bondsman, which is concomitant to forced labour, is the groundwork of the distinctive form of subjectivity which is born in Saint-Domingue.

Building upon Hegel's paradigm, it is fair to claim that the form of self-consciousness that slaves developed via forced labour on Saint-Domingue's plantations is unique because it is equally informed by the system of Vodou practices and beliefs that slaves imported from their African realities. As such, forced labour was intrinsic to the process of imposing Vodou cosmology upon the material and social settings of Saint-Domingue. The slaves overcame their sense of foreignness by being forced into the material production of crops. The formative process is the corollary of being forced into the material production of crops. The continuity of forced labour with Vodou cosmology instilled in the African slaves the conviction of their citizenship as Saint-Dominguois. In other terms, the simplest feeling which determines human agency is the feeling of need, lack of identity or difference from the world, while the simplest form in which human agency dominates or controls its most basic needs is productive labour. Labour presupposes the difference or lack of identity of need, but changes it into a relation, equal and different, by imposing itself and transforming the material world to satisfy the need.[23] However, the experience of slave communities in Saint-Domingue and forced labour fulfil and transcend Hegel's and Rose's paradigms. Even though the products of forced labour remain strictly the privilege of the masters, the slave communities, with the assistance of Vodou cosmology, managed to derive the consciousness of their citizenship and a distinctive form of subjective reality. Social agency and citizenship are outcomes of the slaves' attempt to appropriate Saint-Domingue's physical setting according to guidelines derived from Vodou cosmology.

It is noteworthy that Haitian subjectivity and consciousness of citizenship in Saint-Domingue were born out of slavery. This paradoxical occurrence becomes coherent by acknowledging the spiritual and social intervention of Vodou cosmology in subverting the oppressing and cruel outcomes of slavery in Saint-Domingue and other colonies. C.L.R. James observes, regarding the continuity of the slaves' experience and the uprising in Saint-Domingue, that "working and living together in gangs of hundreds on the huge sugar-factories which covered the North Plain, they [the slaves] were closer to a modern proletariat than any group of workers in existence at the time, and the rising was, therefore, a thoroughly prepared and organized mass movement".[24] Working and living together brought about the implicit awareness among the slaves that both their freedom and salvation depend upon collective effort and cooperation. The slaves acquired their Western social capital through forced labour on the plantations of Saint-Domingue.

Vodou Cosmology, the Lwas and Social Agency

The fact that Vodou is mostly practised in rural places of contemporary Haiti is consistent with its roots on the plantations of Saint-Domingue. The formative activity of labour persists as collective farming among Haitian peasants in the *lakou* agricultural model. Farming is the central activity which reinforces collective relationship among Haitian farmers who are predominantly Vodou adherents. In contemporary Haiti, the Vodou adherent, as a farmer, assumes the role of a social agent through the collective experience of farming. Vodou cosmology and forced labour instilled in Haitian subjectivity that self-realization depends on the realization of the group. *I am unless we are* is one of the fundamental lessons of plantation slavery and Vodou cosmology.

Collective experience is reinforced by the organization and development of the Vodou rituals and farming. The complexity of the rituals is inseparable from the collective experience of farming. The aim of contemporary rituals is to celebrate the Vodou deities. All over Haiti, however, it is agreed that there are two *classes* of deities, the Rada or Arada and the Petro.[25] Social interaction of peasants in the rural context illustrates the norms that the participants derive from the Rada and Petro lwas' rituals. Farming and the Vodou rituals connect every aspect of the peasant's world view to the will of the Vodou lwas. The lwas characterize forces which shape society from underneath.[26] The lwas assume the dual function of spiritual entities and social authorities. Their media of intervention are the Vodou rituals which provide the arena to exercise their authority. Their social authority consists in dictating and defining the social behaviours of the adherents toward each other. Caribbean cosmological systems are complex manifestations of the geographies of crossing and dislocation. They are at the same time manifestations of locatedness, rootedeness and belonging that map individual and collective relationships to the Divine.[27] In the rituals, the lwas mediate a process of interdependence, of mutual beingness, in which one becomes oneself in the process of becoming one with the Sacred, and manifest their sacredness in nature as well as in their relationship with human beings, both of which take shape in a process of mutual embodiment.[28] The social function of contemporary rituals consists in providing an arena for collective interaction in which all the adherents cooperate to prepare the celebration of the lwas. The participants' interactions are regulated by organizing to fulfil the requests of the respective ritual of the lwas. They validate each other as social agents through the collective organization of the rituals while following the requests of the lwas. Hence, in the rituals, the lwas behave as both religious and social mediators among the participants. It is also noteworthy that summoning favours from the lwas during the rituals bears a social implication. Summoning favours from the lwas can be read as a social brokering because the adherent is engaged in negotiation with the lwas who require sacrifices and earthly gifts in order to provide the favours as rewards.

Moreover, the characteristics of some lwas are consistent with the original context of plantation slavery in Saint-Domingue. The harsh characteristics of some lwas reflect the brutal experience of slaves and the hostility of plantation slavery. This fact is plain in the characteristics of the Petro lwas and rituals which are not part of the original ancestral pantheon of the African lwas. Sensitive observation suggests that the elaboration of the Petro lwas' rituals were primarily media of resistance and assimilation in the hostile and brutal circumstances of Saint-Domingue. According to Vodou adherents, the Petro are *plus raide*: harder, tougher, more stern; less tolerant and forgiving; more practical and demanding.[29] As a pantheon of deities, it is obvious that the Petro lwas are a by-product of slavery. The Petro lwas are thus collective creations because they embody the resistance mechanisms of slaves to the violent conditions of slavery and the projection of a collective spiritual reality.

The function of the Petro lwas is defined by the necessity to adjust in Saint-Domingue and coping with the brutality of slavery. These new "American" lwas had a more aggressive approach to problem solving and allowed Haitians to match the violent and aggressive nature of a social order bent toward domination.[30] If pressed, we can infer from Pinn's view that the injunctions of the deities are inseparable from the priestesses' revelations: the deities' injunctions can be known strictly through the priestesses who behave as earthly vehicles of their commands. This fact accentuates the social dimension of Vodou cosmology, which, in absence of a sacred text, must rely on the accounts and deeds of priestesses to be known by the adherents. This process requires effective communication and solidarity in fulfilling the lwas' requests. The dual role of priestesses as both religious vehicles and social seers define a space for the extension of the rituals in the socialization of the adherents.

In Saint-Domingue, the Petro lwas' rituals provided the arena for the slaves to manage their violent proclivities and oppression in a constructive manner. The Petro rituals were efficient in confining violence and aggressiveness to the religious arena; they prevented the eruption of violence and aggressiveness in other aspects of the adherents' social life. As mechanisms of resistance and syncretism, the rituals of Petro lwas are congenial to the collective experience of Vodou cosmology. It is through this process that the religious roles of the participants inform their sociopolitical attitudes. In the Petro rituals, the manifestations of the lwas in daily life depend in great part upon the devotees. That is to say, the direction and intent of cosmic energy is guided by priests, priestesses and devotees who petition for certain effects.[31] Furthermore, the hierarchy among the priests, priestesses and devotees in the Vodou rituals define their religious responsibility and social roles. Assigning religious responsibilities on the basis of hierarchy captures the intersection of the social and spiritual aspects of the rituals. Contemporary Vodou rituals present a complex endeavour in which adherents structure their social reality by relying upon the combination of the lwas' guidelines and social norms. The sacredness of the rituals dwells in the symbolic function of the places in which they occur. By immersing themselves in the rituals, the adherents are simultaneously operating in and outside geographical boundaries. The spiritual connection with the lwas, which is kindled by the rituals, transcends geographical boundaries.

Catholicism, Vodou and the Contest for Haitian Normativity

The syncretism between African deities and ancestral rituals with Catholicism in Saint-Domingue created a competition to define the dominant system of social norms. The inherent social norms and attitudes which underlie the original African practices and those of Catholicism remain antagonistic because of this competition to define social norms. The ongoing competition to set the system of values of Saint-Domingue – and, later, Haitian society – is at the basis of the antagonism between Haitian Vodou and the Catholicism. Both during and after slavery in Saint-Domingue, the Catholic institution sought to censor Vodou practices because its cosmology promotes the social norms and attitudes which are rooted in the African realities of the adherents. Catholicism strives to elaborate a Eurocentric system of norms and values independent of the African realities of the slave communities of Saint-Domingue. As one commentator observes, the goal of the Catholic Church was to further the Western colonialist agenda: "Dans la catéchisation de l'esclave le premier objectif était de faire de la personne du colon une chose sacrée; après quoi tout lui était permis en matière de foi. Voilà comment la religion est mise, plutôt qu'à celui de la charité, au service de l'exploitation coloniale."[32] (The first goal of the catechization of the slave was to consecrate the colonizer, on the basis of which she acquires absolute power. This is how religion is used toward colonial exploitation instead of charity.) In the context of Haiti, the purpose of the Catholic Church was to provide the religious justification of slavery. Catholicism in Saint-Domingue carried out the religious edicts of *Le Code Noir* for the French colonies. As such, Catholicism in Saint-Domingue supplied the religious reinforcement for the slave trade in fulfilling its mission according to the proclamations of *Le Code Noir*.

The open clash between the clergy and vodou practitioners dates back to 1896, when a prominent bishop in Cap-Haïtien led a series of gatherings and meetings under the banner "League against Vodou" in the north, which unsuccessfully sought to win widespread support against vodou.[33] Indeed, Vodou has always been under the threat of extinction and syncretism provided a mechanism for survival, through which it managed to secure its existence. Vodou's religious syncretism with Catholicism is manifest in the Western appearances of its deities. This religious syncretism between Catholic and Vodou norms still thrives among contemporary practitioners who worship both Catholic and Vodou gods while their accompanying norms remain apart. African religions also put down roots in the soil of plantations, changing in the process. They entered into dialogue with the practices of Catholicism, whose saints were imbued with a new meaning by worshippers in both Africa and the Americas.[34] Vodou and the Catholic Church have evolved in unison through syncretism while maintaining the separation of African and Catholic norms. In virtue of their competitive relationship to determine the norms of Haitian identity, Catholic and Vodou practices in Haiti are endemic to the slave context in which they were established. As syncretic religion and a creole cultural form, it was forged out of those traditions in combination with aspects of Amerindian sacred traditions and Catholicism in the New World context of Saint-Domingue, and later Haiti.[35] Following two regimes of norms ascribes a dual social identity to the practitioners.

Furthermore, the syncretic relationship of Catholicism and Vodou is expressed in *Bondye*, who is the godhead in Vodou cosmology. Among Vodou deities, Bondye embodies the Catholic God with African features. Bondye is the synthesis of Vodou and Roman Catholicism. Jean describes a Vodou priest's summon of Bondye in the following: "He implores God by the name of Great Master for assisting him in the execution of his duty. He also pronounces the sacred words of Vodou to obtain the assistance and participation of the Spirits in the ceremony. He sometimes solicits the input of the Divine Savior Jesus Christ to implore God's good graces on him."[36] Calling on both Bondye and the lwas is proof of the inseparability of the Christian godhead and the Vodou deities in Vodou cosmology. As the overseer of all Vodou rituals, Bondye's role expands in the social experience of the practitioners as well. The mediation of Catholic saints with Vodou deities led Zora Neale Hurston to observe during her first-hand study of Haitian Vodou that "even the most illiterate peasant knows that the picture of the saint is only an approximation of the loa".[37] It is thus in assuming both African and Western nature in Vodou cosmology that Bondye reconciles the African heritage of the adherents with their social experience. Even though the specific social norms and values inherent to Vodou and Catholicism are irreconcilable, Bondye's intervention rids the adherent's experience of the ensuing tension in their social reality. Bondye mediates African Voodun and Western Catholicism. Viewed philosophically, in Vodou cosmology, Bondye stands as the synthesis of African and Western religious realities.

The Lwas and Social Norms

The adherents' view of good and evil is coherent with the collective attitude which is inherent to Vodou cosmology. The Rada and Petro, the two pantheons of Vodou deities, inform the ethical attitudes of the adherents. Vodou deities, the loas (or mystères), are multiple and varied. Although generally divided into two main rites or "nations" – the Rada pantheon (of Dahomean or Yoruban origin) and the Petro (creole loas originating principally in Haiti).[38] The deities manifest themselves under either Rada or Petro. For the purpose of my argument, I take Rada and Petro to be two forms under which the deities manifest themselves to adherents. The adherent's ethical proclivity is determined by the revelation of the lwas according to the form that it assumes. The Rada lwas are the "sweet" spirits. They are served with sweet foods and drink. By contrast, the Petro lwas are characterized as "hot" spirits. Their possession performances often play at the border of violence and destructiveness.[39] The rituals thus provide the platform for the lwas to shape the adherent's ethical attitude. This process establishes an isomorphic relation between the adherents' ethical attitude and the form of the lwas. It is indeed important to realize that in Vodou, we find divinities that are yearning to be human. They want to be materially alive, to feel, to suffer or to be happy like the common people.[40] The Vodou deities shape the adherents' ethical attitude in virtue of their anthropomorphic nature. The lwas behave as mediators of the adherents' ethical attitudes via Rada or Petro form. The loa do not correlate with objects in the natural world nor with specific human activities. Instead, their identities are formed by their relation with each other and by their interaction with those they claim as their servitors.[41] The form of the lwas shapes the adherents' perception of good and evil. As central components of Vodou cosmology, the lwas are always shaping the ethical attitudes and experience of the adherents vis-à-vis each other. After all, one god can have many emanations, whether regarded as members of the same family or as different manifestations of the same deity.[42] The mediated relationship of the form of the lwas with the adherent's ethical attitudes defines good and evil as social epithets. It is thus plain that there is a uniform relation between the form of lwas, the adherents' ethical attitude and the interpretation of good and evil by the community of adherents. Consequently, it is through this uniform relation that the lwas shape the moral judgements of the adherents which are reinforced by the community of adherents.

Furthermore, the adherents judge their actions according to their interpretation of the injunctions of the lwas under Petro or Rada form. As Jean Fils-Aimé observes: "L'ordre et le désordre, la vie et la mort, le bien et le mal, les événements heureux ou malheureux, sont mis dans un champ de signification grâce aux lwas, qui font que rien ne peut apparaître absurde à l'individu."[43] (Order and chaos, life and death, good and evil, fortunate and unfortunate events are put into a realm of meanings through the lwas, who make it so that nothing seems to be absurd to the individual.) The injunctions of the lwas thus grant the adherents a cohesive and normative perspective on social reality. In Saint-Domingue, this cohesive outlook made the terrifying aspects of plantation life bearable in providing continuity between the experiences of slave communities with their African context.

It is in framing the adherents' outlook upon good and evil that the lwas inform their ethical experience. The Vodou adherent secures the social recognition of her fellows because ethical behaviours are interpreted according to the lwas' injunctions. Even the best of gods, those of the Rada (Arada) rite from Alladah or Dahomey, can sometimes do evil, while a tough deity like Marinette-Bois-Cheche (Marinette-Dry-Bones) of the Petro rite, known for her bloody behaviour and preference for pimento, gunpowder and gasoline, can be calmed if served properly.[44] So, the lwas reinforce the rationalization of the collective interpretation of good and evil actions in Vodou cosmology. They mediate the adherents' ethical attitudes while securing the consistency and coherence of moral judgements.

However, in conclusion, the role of the lwas makes it difficult to assess autonomy in the ethical experience of the adherents. When viewed from a Western angle, the mediating role of the lwas in the adherents' ethical attitude seems to undermine the adherents' autonomy in postulating the principles of their actions. The issue is that the mediating role of the lwas in the adherents' ethical attitude seems to pose a challenge to freedom of will, as the central constituent of ethical experience. The following chapter takes up the task of elaborating the implications of the mediating role of the lwas in the adherents' ethical attitude for autonomy and freedom of will in the context of Vodou cosmology by contrasting it with Kant's account of the ethical experience.

CHAPTER 2.

Moral Autonomy in Vodou Cosmology and Kant's Ethics

The previous chapter concluded with the claim that in the collective context of Vodou cosmology, the form of the lwas mediates the adherents' ethical attitude and that their injunctions inform their moral judgements, while the prevailing moral judgements of the community of adherents reinforce the deities' injunctions. However, when viewed from the angle of Western ethics, the mediating role of the lwas in the adherents' ethical attitude seems to undermine the adherents' autonomy in supplying the principles of their actions. The issue is that the mediating role of the lwas in the adherents' ethical attitude seems to pose a challenge to freedom of will as the central constituent of ethical experience. This issue raises the following question: How can the adherents' ethical attitude be reconciled with their profile as self-legislated individuals?

Building upon the previous chapter, this chapter argues that moral autonomy and validation are grounded in the community of adherents' reinforcement of moral judgements. Given that in Vodou cosmology, the collective is intrinsically tied to the individual, the moral autonomy of the individual thus depends on the collective reinforcement of the community of adherents. The issue of moral autonomy in Vodou cosmology is pertinent to the Enlightenment because it delineates how slave communities in Saint-Domingue define their moral autonomy vis-à-vis oppressive institutions in similar fashion as the Enlightenment centred on assisting Westerners in overcoming the clergy's dogmatism throughout Europe. As chapter 1 shows, forced labour instilled the plural pronoun "we" as the marker of a pluralistic subjectivity among slave communities. My argument is that as an extension of this pluralistic subjectivity among slaves, moral autonomy is accordingly pluralistic instead of individualistic, which is articulated in the moral autonomy of Westerners. On the basis of forced labour and Vodou cosmology, the practitioner asserts her moral autonomy via the collective.

To elaborate my argument that moral autonomy and validation are grounded in the community of adherents' reinforcement of moral judgements, I draw out kinship between aspects of the adherent's ethical experience and some key concepts of the Enlightenment discourse about ethics presented in Kant's *Foundations of the Metaphysics of Morals* (1785) and *Critique of Practical Reason* (1788). In these texts, Kant grapples with similar aspects of the ethical experience of Westerners. Drawing an analogy between Haitian Vodou adherents' ethical attitude and Kant's discourse about Westerners is pragmatic because it makes some unfamiliar aspects of the Vodou's adherent's ethical experience more comprehensible to readers who are not acquainted with the dynamics of Haitian Vodou. Also, it contributes to situating the discussion of subjectivity in Saint-Domingue within the larger context of the Enlightenment. The comparison aims at showing that understanding the ethical experience, in the context of Vodou cosmology, requires a collective conceptualization of freedom in lieu of Kant's transcendental account of freedom as the starting point of ethical experience. On the basis of the comparison, I will conclude that this collective account of freedom offers an alternative to Kant's analysis of moral autonomy and transcendental freedom. However, a full elaboration of Kant's ethics is beyond the scope of this section.

Reasonableness, Obligation and Universality

I will now draw out the concepts of Kant's ethics that are pertinent to my argument. Kant's moral philosophy unfolds upon the assertion of transcendental freedom. That is the idea that freedom from sensory-based constraints and commitment to the moral law allows the will to be unconditionally good. Kant is interested in the conditions that make the expression of freedom possible according to the moral law. Put differently, transcendental freedom requires overcoming the passions and inclinations which sometimes determine the decisions of individuals in moral matters. Once the individual's will is extricated from these constraints, it ought to follow the edict of the moral law, which guarantees its non-partiality and cohesiveness.

This fact is proof that Kant understands the aim of moral philosophy as an investigation of the relation of freedom and practical reason to create an unconditionally good will. For Kant, the unconditional good is intrinsically tied with freedom of will's mediation by the moral law. There is thus an isomorphic relationship between the unconditional good and the will's fitness to transcend the passions and inclinations. This isomorphic relationship between freedom of the will and the unconditional good is achievable through the mediation of the moral law; the moral law behaves as the guarantor of cohesive ethical experiences.

In this context, the moral law as the vehicle of practical reason works in tandem with the will to realize the unconditional good. Indeed for Kant, reason, in its practical application, has only one goal: to lead the will toward the moral law and self-determination. In ethics, it (freedom) turns out to be none other than practical (moral) freedom: self-determination. Free of all causation and external influence, the will establishes the law for itself.[1] The will is a formal entity; it only provides the form of the principles that guide the individual's actions. Moral autonomy thus depends on compliance with the will's principles. For Kant, the will is free only upon the condition that its regulating principles are bound by practical reason. Accordingly, a will that creates principles independently of the moral law is constrained; it is a conditional will. For Kant, such will is bound by the vagaries of external conditions and the inclinations of self-love. Moreover, a bound will is irrational because it operates according to principles that are determined by external circumstances and are beyond the boundaries of the moral law. In Kant's words: "Therefore the preeminent good can consist only in the conception of law in itself (which can be present only in a rational being) so far as this conception and not the hoped-for effect is the determining ground of the will."[2]

Kant's statement articulates the constellation of the central concepts of his moral philosophy. The cohesive relationship of freedom, law and will expresses the uniformity of the central themes of his moral philosophy.

Kant confirms such unity in the claim that "freedom and unconditional practical law reciprocally imply each other".[3] The unconditional good nature of the will depends on its isomorphic relation with freedom and practical law. Freedom, as Kant understands it, is a special kind of causality, unconditioned by any prior cause. As we will see, freedom of the will is important to Kant not merely for the familiar reason that we cannot be held accountable if we are not free, but because it provides both the content of morality and its motive.[4] Freedom of the will and moral autonomy are fundamental constituents of morality for Kant. Self-regulation in agreement with the moral law presupposes freedom of will while simultaneously reinforcing such freedom. Hence, freedom is the starting point of moral experience while being both its content and goal, as well. From Kant's angle, freedom is absurd without a specific set of norms to regulate its expression. On this account, far from being incompatible with constraint, freedom consists in a distinctive kind of constraint: constraint by norms. This sounds paradoxical but it is not. The positive freedom Kant is describing is the practical capacity to be bound by discursive norms.[5] Imposing constrains upon the will and abiding by them are essential dimensions of moral experience and freedom in Kant's moral philosophy.

The will's agreement with the moral law guarantees its freedom and that of other agents as well. The community of free self-regulated agents creates what Christine Korsgaard calls the "kingdom of ends". To act reasonably and universally is the outcome of the autonomy that each agent enjoys as a self-regulated individual. Being reasonable and universal is achievable via the will's compliance with the moral law. A rational will is simultaneously a universal will because practical law derives its power to guide the will from its universality. For Kant, the essential character of the moral law is universality. Therefore, the person who acts from duty attends to the universality of their principle. They only act on a maxim that they could will to be a universal law.[6] As a means to preserve both the autonomy and sociality of the will, Kant asserts that universality is the form of the moral law. The universal nature of the moral law thus assumes a strategic purpose in Kant's moral philosophy. Universality reconciles individual will with other wills and assures their cohesion. Kant asserts the ideal of the moral law in stating: "So act that the maxim of your will could always hold at the same time as a principle in a giving of universal law."[7] Universality is thus an essential dimension of the will. It is through universality as an inherent dimension of the moral law that a singular will can engage rationally in the community of wills. This fact is central to Kant's moral philosophy and will be later contrasted with the adherent's ethical experience in the context of Vodou cosmology. For Kant, the will starts with the conviction of its own freedom and then proceeds to deduce the freedom of other wills. The assumption that other wills can act as my will indirectly asserts that they must be as free as my own will. So, for Kant, the will transcends the singularity of its freedom and infers the freedom of other wills in complying with the intrinsic universality of the moral law. Universality overcomes the apparent obstacles of rational validation and moral autonomy. It will be shown, in contrast, that under Vodou cosmology, the fact that collective freedom is at the basis of individual freedom makes the judgement of other adherents an inherent aspect of the adherent's ethical experience.

Kant is emphatic upon the autonomy of the will. To preserve its independence from external influences and subjective principles, Kant calls for the test of one's principles according to the requirement of the moral law. Besides preserving the consistency of the will with universality, this requirement is meant to guarantee the will's consistency with its own principles and to rule out contradictions in their social application. The necessity to fulfil the universal requirement of the moral law guarantees the unconditional goodness of the will and its consistency with other wills to the extent that their maxims are rational. However, at this juncture, Kant acknowledges the circularity between freedom, universality and self-legislation. He states: "This is circular because freedom and self-legislation of the will are both autonomy and thus are reciprocal concepts, and for that reason one of them cannot be used to explain the other and to furnish a ground for it."[8] Kant then preserves the consistency of the will's freedom with the moral law and universality and ends the circularity in claiming that "the concept of obligation to extend the maxim of my self-love to the happiness of others as well."[9] The concept of obligation links one's will to other wills; it is the conceptual apparatus for the universality of the moral law. An individual will partakes in intersubjectivity in fulfilling the duty that the concept of obligation entails. However, Kant goes on to warn: "The direct opposite of the principle of morality is the principle of one's own happiness made the determining ground of the will."[10] So, the concept of obligation articulates the intervention of practical reason to preserve the continuity of one's will with other wills. As a duty, the concept of obligation extricates the will from the circular relationship of freedom and self-legislation while acknowledging other wills in the formulation of its principles.

The concept of obligation highlights the impossibility of asserting one's freedom of will unless there is adequate ground for its cohesion with other wills. For Kant, it is impossible to achieve conviction of one's freedom of will on theoretical grounds because it is essentially an idea of reason. In Kant's words: "We have finally reduced the definite concept of morality to the Idea of freedom, but we could not prove freedom to be actual in ourselves and in human nature."[11] Freedom requires both universality and objective expressions to be deemed real. The fact that the purpose of universality and objectivity is the concrete realization of freedom suggests that for Kant, freedom of the will is an axiom of morality which depends upon its cohesion with other wills under the watchful guidance of the moral law.

Another necessary step in the will's relationship with other wills is the acknowledgement that they are equally free. However, there is a conundrum in the fact that if the freedom of my will and self-legislation share a circular relationship and are theoretical in nature, how can one confidently assert such freedom for other wills? In other words, I can only be cognizant of the freedom of my own will. The way out of this riddle is to acknowledge other wills' freedom on the basis of their conformity with the principles of the moral law. Prior to such acknowledgement, one can merely assume the freedom of other wills. Kant delineates how to acknowledge the freedom of other wills in the following statement:

> Now I affirm that we must necessarily grant that every rational being who has a will also has the Idea of freedom and that it acts only under this Idea. For in such a being we think of a reason which is practical (i.e. a reason which has causality with respect to its object). Now we cannot conceive of a reason which, in making its judgments, consciously responds to a bidding from the outside, for then the subject would attribute the determination of its power of judgment not to reason but to an impulse.[12]

So, the proof of other wills' freedom stands on two axes. First, it has to act in such a way to make it evident to other wills that it is following the moral law. Secondly, it has to display its autonomy by not succumbing to the pressures of impulses and external circumstances when formulating its principles of actions.

Following principles of actions that agree with the moral law is proof of the freedom of one's will and that of other wills. The community of wills thus shares a cohesive relationship under the common guidance of the moral law and the principles of actions which confirm their freedom. Furthermore, formulating principles for specific actions confirms the reality of freedom and morality. It is in assessing whether specific acts are good or evil – whether they comply with the moral law or not – that the community of wills fulfils Kant's concept of reasonableness. For Kant: "What we are to call good must be an object of the faculty of desire in the judgment of every reasonable human being, and evil an object of aversion to the eyes of everyone; hence for this appraisal reason is needed, in addition to sense."[13] In this claim, Kant posits an intrinsic association between good, evil and reasonableness. As a constellation, good, evil and reasonableness unfold under the watchful gaze of practical reason. Thus, what is reasonable depends on the intersubjective agreement of wills which approves a given act as good. Evil is a violation of the cohesion of wills and unreasonable because it fails to secure the approval of the community of wills. Kant's account of reasonableness suggests that it promotes the objective realization of practical reason in the concrete realm, since the formal nature of practical reason requires the harmonious relationship of wills under the moral law and universality in order to become reasonable. Hence, reasonable actions are both the manifestation and expansion of practical reason in the social realm; practical reason partakes in intersubjectivity as it complies with reasonable principles.

Kant's account of reasonableness reconciles the transcendental nature of the will's freedom with the community of wills. Being reasonable bridges one's freedom of will with the community of wills. Thus, it has a sociable role because Kant acknowledges that practical reason is inclined to pursue its own self-interests and welfare when driven by the faculty of desire. When that happens, reason succumbs to self-love, which is a pathological expression of happiness. This is why Kant is emphatic upon the necessity to restrict the natural tendency to indulge in self-love. He states: "Pure practical reason merely infringes upon self-love, inasmuch as it only restricts it, as natural and active in us even prior to the moral law, to the condition of agreement with this law, and then it is called rational self-love."[14] It is noteworthy that Kant formulates rational self-love and reasonableness as twin concepts. Loving oneself rationally implies the adoption of a reasonable attitude by the will in a specific community of wills. Kant's account suggests that the main issue with natural self-love is that it is fundamentally unreasonable. Rational self-love is essentially the ability of the will to freely impose norms upon itself while being confident that its norms are reconcilable with those of other wills. It is what Brandom summarizes as the symmetry of authority and responsibility in Kant's moral philosophy: "So Kant's normative conception of positive freedom is of freedom as a kind of authority. Specifically, it consists in our authority to make ourselves rationally responsible by taking ourselves to be responsible. . . . Here authority and responsibility are symmetric and reciprocal, constitutive features of the normative subject who is at once authoritative and responsible."[15]

Hitherto, we have seen that freedom of the will – the starting point of Kant's moral philosophy – is transcendental and circular. It transcends its circularity through the universal requirement of the moral law and the concepts of obligation and reasonableness. Obligation and reasonableness are thus best understood as sociable media through which the will reconciles its freedom with that of other wills. Now that I have outlined the concepts in Kant's ethics that are pertinent to my argument – namely, obligation and reasonableness – I will now go on to argue that the Vodou adherents' process of reconciling their individual wills with those of other members of the community is similar to Kant's strategy as it is laid out in the concepts of obligation and reasonableness.

Vodou Lwas and the Universality of Ethical Experience

The structure of the will's freedom, as the basis of the ethical experience in Vodou cosmology, is collective. The collective nature of the will is the outcome of two key aspects in the adherent's experience. First, plantation slavery in Saint-Domingue gave rise to a collective conception of freedom in slave communities. The material circumstances of the Vodou adherent's will were not conducive to its formal relation with freedom as prescribed by the Enlightenment's paradigm, which is illustrated in Kant's discourse about ethics. The elaboration of freedom, as a collective phenomenon among slave communities of Saint-Domingue, gives an alternative outlook on freedom, which is coherent with the circumstances of the transatlantic slave trade. Also, it provides a subtle critique of Kant's formal and individual account of freedom, by suggesting that a collective view of freedom is equally fit to shape the will. Consequently, the elaboration of slaves' subjectivity in Saint-Domingue which is shaped by this collective outlook on freedom provides an alternative frame of subjectivity.

After all, transcendental freedom is an idea of reason; it is in essence theoretical. The conditions of slavery were not favourable to a theoretical conception of freedom. The ethical experience of the adherents depended on the approval of their fellows and the injunctions of the lwas, which is the basis of freedom. The collective view of freedom is born out of the restrains of slavery. Also, it is noteworthy that the Vodou deities' injunctions are, in Kantian speak, the unconditional dimensions of slave communities' ethical experience. The deities' injunctions are unconditional because they do not depend on the external circumstances of the slaves' daily life. This collective nature of freedom of will is both akin and differs from Kant's account in calling for a collective approach to moral autonomy.

Understanding the role of the lwas in the ethical experience of the adherents requires acknowledgement of their dual role as historical and spiritual entities in the experience of the adherents. The centrality of the lwas as both historical and spiritual entities lies in the fact that their initial function was to be the media for cohesive and meaningful bonding among the communities of slaves who came from different African realities. Indeed, as previously discussed, Vodou initially evolved as a means to overcome social dissonance, namely the experience of isolation and estrangement of the slaves in Saint-Domingue. Vodou established the sense of common social destiny among uprooted slaves from different parts of Africa. All these Negroes brought from Africa – Peuhl warriors, Mondongues, the mighty Mandingues, tall Yoloffs, Ibos, Bamabaras, Dahomeans – eliminated little by little their intertribal differences and were able to form a fighting unity through the medium of Vodou, an ensemble of beliefs and rites of African origin, subsequently becoming closely mingled with Catholic practices.[16] What Lemoine omits, in the above observation, is that the gradual elimination of intertribal differences was feasible upon ongoing negotiation of ethical and social norms. This negotiation of ethical and social norms elaborated the social infrastructure of the later free Saint-Domingue. The slaves overcame their marginality in Saint-Domingue while validating each other as ethical agents. In the rituals, the lwas provide the injunctions which the adherents negotiate in order to create their ethical and social principles. It is by supplying the injunctions, which are enacted as social and ethical principles, that the lwas shape the social experience of the adherents. The appearance of the gods and even the cult of the ancestors, are operative only in a social world: the spirits are always, for better or for worse, functions of rather exigent – though sometimes temporary – sociopolitical situations.[17] During their appearance, they behave as both mediator and legislator of the adherents' freedom of will vis-à-vis each other. The lwas thus provide both the content of the ethical principles and the social goal of ethical experience.

The lwas grounds the adherents' will in the unity of the ethical practices of the community. Initially, the intervention of the lwas was necessary to overcome the difference in ethical perspectives given the diverse tribal backgrounds of the slaves. It is in virtue of their function as neutralizers of ethical differences that the lwas are the basis of the adherents' freedom of will. In contrast to Kant's account, the Vodou adherent's freedom is inseparable from the experience of slavery and the intervention of the lwas to establish the sociability and reasonableness of their will. The universal and reasonable component of the adherents' will comes from the function of the lwas as neutralizer of ethical differences and supplier of social and ethical principles. The role of the lwas is thus unison with the collectivity inherent to freedom of will in Vodou cosmology.

It is in being the basis of freedom of will that the lwas stand as the unconditioned dimension of the adherent's will. Concretely, the lwas mediate the adherents' will through their manifestations which determine the ethical modalities of the moral experience. These manifestations in the rituals are objective expressions of the adherent's freedom. The Vodou lwas are thus to the adherent's will what freedom is to the agent's will in Kant's ethics. As the synthesis of the adherents' freedom of will, they are the starting point of the causal structure in ethical experience. It is safe to think that the lwas kindle the spontaneity of the adherent's will. Spontaneity, in Kant's usage, is the capacity to deploy concepts. Deploying concepts is making judgements and endorsing practical maxims.[18] The lwas stand as the synthesis of the freedom of the adherents to the extent that they mediate while assuring the cohesion of each adherent's ethical principles with her fellow. A living proof of the extension of the lwas' injunctions in the social experience of practitioners is available in the role of the *chef de section*, a rural administrator who functions as both a Vodou priest and social mediator. As a social mediator, the duty of the *chef de section* is to reconcile the national government's laws with the prevailing norms of the given village while abiding by the lwas' injunctions. Wade Davis describes the tripartite function of the *chef de section*, as Vodou priest, social mediator and rural administrator, in the following:

> To reach these people [rural peasants] the national authorities depend on one man, *the chef de section*, an appointee from within the *section rurale* who is expected to establish networks of contacts that will place eyes and ears in every lakou under his jurisdiction. Typically he maintains his own field, is polygynous, and serves the loa. In many instances he is a prominent houngan (Vodou priest). It is his task, after all, to investigate conflicts and convene the informal tribunals at which virtually all local disputes are said to be resolved.[19]

Davis's description of the *chef de section* suggests a paradigm of the Vodou adherent as an individual who is regulated by Haitian governmental norms and the lwas' injunctions. In virtue of the lwas' injunctions, the adherent operates simultaneously as Vodou faithful and social agent.

Furthermore, the lwas oversee the collective process of creating ethical principles and grants them the universal requirement that Kant posits for practical reason. In following the injunctions of the lwas to create ethical principles, the adherents commit to the requirement of Kant's categorical imperative, namely the ideal to act in such a way that if everyone were to act similarly there would be no contradiction and would yield a universal law. This is illustrated in the fact that in order to receive the lwas' injunctions, the Vodou priestess or *hounsi kanzo* "must have a mastery of [herself], be prepared to receive the loa and, most of all, to localize and control what for the uninitiated remains vague or unreal."[20] The function of the deities in shaping the will is confirmed in the collective ethical experience of the adherents. The loa cannot appear in an epiphany, cannot be made manifest on earth without the person who becomes the temporary receptacle of mount. The possessed gives themselves up to become an instrument in a social and collective drama.[21]

The lwas' injunctions become available to all participants in this social and collective event. This religious and social event conditions the participants to behave reasonably; they derive their ethical norms from this African-based reality. Complying with the injunctions of the lwas fulfils the requirement of reasonableness, in Kant's account, because they provide the collective dimension of the ethical experience in Vodou cosmology.

However, a key difference is that for Kant, the categorical imperative and transcendental freedom are formal. In contrast, the process through which the adherents derive the deities' injunction is a collective and social event. It is noteworthy that the collective nature of freedom is consistent with the experience of slavery in which slaves are continuously compelled to prioritize the welfare of the group over their individual welfare. The inherent collectivity of freedom is thus the by-product of survival technologies in slave communities. C.L.R. James makes the following observation regarding collective experience and Vodou: "By hard experience they [slaves] had learnt that isolated efforts were doomed to failure, and in the early months of 1792 in and around Le Cap they were organized for revolution. Voodoo was the medium of the conspiracy."[22] It is safe to infer from James's observation that the Kantian model of autonomy and self-legislation was not a suitable model for slave communities. In positing Vodou as a medium of conspiracy, James acknowledges the social prowess of its practices in neutralizing private interests in favour of collective aims.

The realization of the futility of self-oriented efforts by the slaves is the basis of the collective nature of freedom among Vodou adherents in a slave-based society. Such collective realization of the nature of freedom coincides with Kant's account of universality, as well. Consequently, the adherents fulfil the Enlightenment's ideals and Kant's concepts of obligation and the reasonable in deriving the suitable ethical norms to guide their social interactions through an experience of freedom which is collective. Moreover, the inherent collectivity which emerges out of forced labour assists the ethical experience of slave communities in fulfilling Kant's concept of obligation while freeing them from the circularity of Kant's ethics. As slaves, the adherents of Vodou behaved reasonably in collective cooperation to guarantee their self-preservation. Grasping the necessity of collective cooperation, as a mechanism for survival, yields collective consciousness, which parallels Kant's concept of obligation.

Reasonable and Unreasonable as Modalities of the Lwas

In Vodou cosmology, the ethical experience occurs through the interaction of freedom of will and the mediation of the lwas' injunctions. The fact that "the same Lwa may appear as Rada and as Petwo[, a]nd what seems to distinguish the Rada pantheon from the Petwo pantheon is, above all, the general character, attitude, or persona of the Lwa"[23] suggests that Rada and Petwo may be interpreted as the modalities that the lwas choose to assume for their manifestation. The mediation of the ethical principles and the adherent's will happens through the modality the lwas assume as Rada and Petro to become manifest. The social extension of Rada and Petro happens through the ethical modalities that they avail to the adherents. The Rada lwas are the "sweet" spirits. They are served with sweet foods and drink. The Petro lwas, by contrast, are characterized as "hot" spirits. Their possession performances often play at the border of violence and destructiveness.[24]

It is thus accurate to view Rada as the modality through which the deities call upon the adherents to behave reasonably. The Petro modality, on the other hand, summons anti-collective behaviours. The Vodou rituals are then the arenas through which the adherent's will complies with the deities' injunctions to be reasonable or unreasonable. This process leads to a symmetrical relationship between the adherent's will and the manifestation of the lwas. As the deities, the lwas are initially neutral forces. Rada and Petro provide the modalities they assume to assist the adherents in creating social and ethical principles. Thus, this is how Rada and Petro supply the ethical modalities which determine the reasonable and antisocial attitudes of the adherents. As an ethical modality, Rada encompasses reasonableness and is the source of principles that secure collective approval. On the other hand, self-loving principles that fail the requirements of reasonableness fall under Petro.

Furthermore, the agreement of behaviours with either the Petro or Rada modality of the lwas parallels Kant's account of good and evil. Consider, for example, Kant's statement that "what we are to call good must be an object of the faculty of desire in the judgment of every reasonable human being, and evil an object of aversion to the eyes of everyone; hence for this appraisal reason is needed, in addition to sense".[25] Rada modality coincides with Kant's account of the good because it is the source of principles that are approved by the community of adherents. Petro modality illustrates evil in triggering anti-collective principles of actions. *Lwa Rada* are assumed to be kind and benevolent whereas *Lwa Petro* are harsh and demanding.[26] In Vodou cosmology, an action is deemed good when it secures collective approval and follows Rada modality. Self-loving actions are evil and follow Petro modality.

Theolepsy and the Universality of Ethical Experience

The agreement of the will with the lwas' injunctions assumes physical manifestation in the event of theolepsy. In Vodou rituals, theolepsy occurs when the adherent's body becomes possessed by the lwas' manifestation as Rada or Petro. Theolepsy contributes to the ethical experience of the adherents because it is the physical expression of the mediation of the will by the lwas' injunctions. In theolepsy, the spirit is called into the head of either the houngan (Vodou priest) or an assistant and, like an oracle, the physical body of man dispenses the knowledge of the gods.[27] Theoleptic experience is the physical event through which the adherent's will assumes Petro or Rada as ethical modalities. This fact presents an additional difference between the ethical experience under Vodou cosmology and Kant's ethical model. For Kant, the occurrence of the ethical experience usually remains a private and reflective experience. In the occurrence of the ethical experience, for Kant, the body ought not to show any physical expression of the ethical experience. Kant allows only the feelings of pleasure and displeasure as attendants of the will's agreement with the moral law: "Hence we can see a priori that the moral law, as the determining ground of the will, must by thwarting all our inclinations produce a feeling that can be called pain; and here we have the first and perhaps the only case in which we can determine a priori from concepts the relation of a cognition (here a cognition of pure practical reason) to the feeling of pleasure and displeasure."[28] Any explicit display of the ethical experience is, for Kant, a transgression of the autonomy of the will by pathological-external circumstances. To preserve its formality, the will's compliance with the moral law must refrain from any manifestation.

The occurrence of theolepsy, on the other hand, preserves the African inheritance of the adherent's ethical experience. The fact that the agreement of the will with the lwas' injunctions assumes corporeal expression is consistent with the conception of freedom prevalent in slave-based communities. Theolepsy captures the concrete expression of collective freedom given the role of the lwas as the source of spiritual and social cohesion among displaced slaves. Also, theoleptic experience is congenial to mutual recognition in that it provides palpable assurance to the adherents of the common source of their principles of actions. Another implication of theolepsy lies in the fact that the physical assumption of the Petro and Rada as ethical modalities by the adherents includes both the physical and rational faculties. The possessed body is a mediator between the intimacy of the personal and the cultural symbols, between the past and the present; it is the instrument for the mirroring of self through the spirits, spirits that are at the same time collective and individual.[29]

Indeed, it is on the basis of theoleptic experience that the possessed adherent secures the recognition of her fellows as both a religious faithful and ethical messenger. The adherent's possessed body provides tangible record of the deities' injunctions. Mutual recognition is concomitant to the collective attitude in Vodou cosmology because, historically, it was mandatory for the inclusion of dispersed slaves in a common sociopolitical context. Establishing mutual recognition was the essential medium for the transcendence of tribal differences among slaves. Indeed, the fact that the pantheon of the lwas initially functioned as the spiritual and social means in overcoming the heterogeneity of mores among slaves that resulted from national and tribal differences provides another difference between the ethical experience in Vodou and that of Kant. Kant's moral account can assert an isomorphic relationship between freedom of will and the moral law on the ground of homogeneity of values and norms among Europeans. Such homogeneity of values and norms derives from centuries of coexistence in free societies and the absence of tribal differences among Westerners.

However, the physical dimension that the ethical experience inherits through theolepsy seems to make it susceptible to the issue of rational validity, which Kant avoids by confining the ethical experience to the domain of pure practical reason. Kant is emphatic upon the independence of the ethical experience from external vagaries in order to preserve the consistency, predictability and repetition of the ethical experience, which preserve its universality. His incentive for delineating the ethical experience strictly within the rational domain is to guarantee the consistent repetition and universality of the moral law. The issue that external incentives and expressions pose for the ethical experience is that they undermine the likeliness of the repetition and universality of the moral law.

On the other hand, the rational validity of the ethical experience, under Vodou cosmology, presupposes a collective conception of freedom. Theoleptic experience reinforces this collective conception of freedom in making it concretely available to the community of adherents. Thus, the adherent's ethical experience is validated rationally through theoleptic experience because it is consistent with the prevailing conception of freedom under Vodou cosmology, whereas, in Kant's account, the fact that ethical experience is independent from external influences and expression is consistent with its starting point in transcendental freedom. Ethical experience in Vodou cosmology, on the other hand, achieves rational validity through theolepsy as a collective experience, which in involving every participant, secures consistency and predictability of the adherent's ethical principles. The fact that all the adherents are susceptible to experiencing theolepsy preserves the consistency and repetition of their ethical principles. The physical dimension of the ethical experience supplies the cohesion and universality of ethical experience in Vodou cosmology.

In conclusion, the collective conception of freedom and the physical dimension of the ethical experience delineate an alternative to reach universality and rational validity beside Kant's concepts of obligation and reasonableness to secure the universality of the will. Also, it illustrates core components of slaves' subjectivity in Saint-Domingue, which emerged in kinship and contrast to the ideals of the Enlightenment. Indeed, it is by delineating such an alternative that the collective conception of freedom, in Vodou cosmology, meets and expands the Kantian Enlightenment's account of transcendental freedom and moral autonomy. In spite of their dissimilarities, the community between Vodou cosmology and Kant's ethical discourse lies in the project of forging subjectivities under different social circumstances of the Enlightenment.

CHAPTER 3.

Hegel and Buck-Morss on the Misrecognition of Haitian Vodou's Contribution to the Haitian Revolution

The goal of this chapter is twofold. First, it argues that Hegel's omission of the significance of the Haitian Revolution in both the *Phenomenology of Spirit* (1807) and the introduction to *The Philosophy of History* (1822, 1830–31) is deliberate and that this deliberate omission is the implication of his depiction of sub-Saharan African religious rituals through Protestant philosophical constructs in his *Philosophy of History*. Hegel's Protestant biased philosophical constructs against Africans and their religious reality blinded him to the inherent collective prowess of their religious reality, which made the Haitian Revolution possible. These Protestant philosophical biases and his hostility toward Africans' religious reality lead Hegel to depict the rich and complex religious practices of sub-Saharan Africans as mere chaos and idolatry. Hegel relies on this depiction to fashion Africans as "Negroes" – Godless, barbaric, cruel and whose disposition makes enslavement their natural merit. It is in virtue of this carefully crafted strategy to delineate Africans as barbaric and the inferior other of Europeans that Hegel provides a conceptual means to the transatlantic slave trade. Ultimately, under Hegel's philosophical pen, Africans and people of African descent are classed as a people whose main contribution to Western culture was slavery or to have availed themselves as mere tools of wealth production.

Second, this chapter argues that despite Hegel's tardy acknowledgement of Haiti as a sovereign state, in *Philosophy of Mind* (1845), he nevertheless fails to recognize the import of African religious reality to Vodou in Saint-

Domingue. Instead, in keeping with his Protestant biased philosophical constructs, Hegel misrecognizes Haiti as a Christian nation. As a prop to elaborate these arguments, I engage with Susan Buck-Morss's account of the situation of the Haitian Revolution and Haiti in Hegel's corpus to show that like Hegel, Buck-Morss overlooks the collective disposition of Haitian Vodou as its distinctive import to the Haitian Revolution in comparing it to the practices of Freemasonry. Even though Buck-Morss argues accurately that Hegel was aware of the Haitian Revolution and that it influenced his rendition of the Lord and Bondsman dialectic in the *Phenomenology of Spirit*, I desist from Buck-Morss's view that Hegel did not discuss the Haitian Revolution explicitly because of his dire social and financial circumstances during the completion of the *Phenomenology of Spirit*. Instead, I propose that Hegel deliberately excluded any explicit discussion of the intricacies of the Haitian Revolution because his Protestant biased philosophical constructs against Africans and African religious reality confined him to viewing Africans and people of African descent in Saint-Domingue as inherently unfit to undertake such a large-scale revolt.

Protestant Philosophy as Methodology

In the lectures of *Philosophy of History*, Hegel sets out to provide a universal account of history which transcends what he holds to be the inherent limitations of the traditional methods of historical research. In the introduction to the lectures, it is apparent that Hegel's goal is twofold. First, he engages in a critique of historical methodology. Second, after drawing out the shortcomings of this methodology, Hegel provides an historical account of world events by positing that world history ought to unfold along a temporal-geographical axis. In his mind, one of the inherent limitations of traditional historical research is its lack of universality, which results from failing to espouse a temporal-geographical research approach. The philosophical import of Hegel's undertaking lies in the attempt to elaborate the logical continuity of historical events irrespectively of their different temporal and geographical contexts, which in turns secures universality. Universality consists in the logical continuity of world historical events. Universal history seeks unity and coherence of historical events, which may seem discontinuous to traditional methods of historical research. Accordingly, Hegel claims the distinctiveness of his endeavour upon its suitability to show the logical continuity of historical events that seem incoherent. He thinks philosophy the suitable discipline for this undertaking because it is sensitive to the unfolding of reason in world history on the premises of historical events; drawing out the unfolding of reason through historical events provides proof of the inherent continuity of what may seem random to traditional historians. In Hegel's words: "The only thought which Philosophy brings with it to the contemplation of History is the simple conception of Reason; that Reason is the Sovereign of the World; that the history of the world, therefore, presents us with a rational process."[1] By positing Reason as the "Sovereign" of the world, Hegel rules out what may seem random in world history. The rational dimension of world history lies in the logical necessity that makes world events a coherent system. In positing logical necessity at the core of world history, Hegel thereby commits his rendition to historical teleology. There has to be a telos, an ultimate end toward which the logic of world history unfolds. Hegel elaborates this teleology as follows: "That this 'Idea' or 'Reason' is the True, the Eternal, the absolutely powerful essence; that it reveals itself in the World, and that in that World nothing else is revealed but this and its honor and glory – is the thesis which, as we have said, has been proven in Philosophy, and is here regarded as demonstrated."[2]

This passage elucidates the methodological process of Hegel's project. After distinguishing it from traditional historical investigations, he emphasizes that philosophy contributes to history via the instrumental role of reason in interpreting world history. Also, the above statement introduces the religious premise of Hegel's philosophical account of world history. For Hegel, the philosophy of history is the process which deduces reason as the unmoved mover of the substance of the world. Hegel will locate art, religion and philosophy at the level of absolute spirit.[3] Hegel reinforces the religious basis of his project by associating historical events with providence. He states:

> On the contrary our earnest endeavor must be directed toward the recognition of the ways of Providence, the means it uses, and the historical phenomena in which it manifests itself; and we must show their connection with the general principle above mentioned. . . . I have been unwilling to leave out of sight the connection between our thesis – that Reason governs and has governed the

World – and the question of the possibility of a knowledge of God, chiefly that I might not lose the opportunity of mentioning the imputation against Philosophy of being shy of noticing religious truths, or of having the occasion to be so; in which is insinuated the suspicion that it has anything but a clear conscience in the presence of these truths.[4]

This passage makes it plain that the logical process which unfolds through history is coherent with the Christian concept of providence. Hegel's espousal of logical necessity draws out Christian providence from world historical events as well. The guiding concepts of reason, in the context of Hegel's investigation, are geared toward the revelation of God's knowledge as "the ways of providence". Hegel's philosophy held on to the Christian teleology of a divine plan. His philosophy explicitly affirmed Protestantism in the guise of reason.[5] According to Hegel's reading, philosophy turns out to be inextricably linked with Protestant theology by conflating logical necessity with providence as the guiding principle.

For Hegel, providence is the rational articulation of God's being according to logical necessity. Hegel associates this world-mind with "divine providence". Sure enough, God makes his final appearance shortly afterwards in "Absolute Mind".[6] Moreover, by chastising philosophy for its shyness toward religious truths, Hegel makes it plain that he is critical of both history and philosophy. The former fails to appreciate the logical continuity and necessity of world events. The latter fails to acknowledge that the manifestation of God's will according to logical necessity constitutes reason. Hegel reprimands philosophy for not appreciating the "ways of Providence" as the necessity of Reason. Philosophy and history fail to be receptive to the uniform expression of God's being in historical events. At this juncture, there is confirmation that Hegel's interpretation of the dominant periods and events of world history will follow a Protestant philosophical methodology. Hegel goes on to assert that the Oriental, Greek, Roman and German worlds are the historical periods in which providence is manifest as historical events. The Oriental world is the starting point, and the rise of the German world is the zenith in the process of providence's revelation. It is noteworthy that Hegel does not acknowledge the African world as a period of world history.

From this perspective, Hegel regards history as the suitable arena to behold the revelation of providence through a logical process. Hegel seeks to improve upon the Christian conception of providence by arguing that we should not rest content with "a retail view" of the nature of providence but that our faith in providence should be applied to the whole.[7] God's self-revelation through world history takes the form of Spirit. For Hegel, the unfolding of world history maps out the evolution of Spirit toward absolute knowledge. "Universal history is exclusively occupied with showing how Spirit comes to a recognition and adoption of the Truth: the dawn of knowledge appears; it begins to discover salient principles, and at last arrives at full consciousness."[8] History merely chronicles the empirical expression of Spirit as it ascends to "full consciousness". Only philosophy is adequate to be sensitive to the logical unity of world history. For Hegel, it is in virtue of its logical elaboration that Spirit grants universality to world history. Hegel is trying to develop a notion of historical events as events which have an internal (that is, a nonchance) connection which is unlike the internal connection of natural law or nature gives to events.[9] The Oriental, Greek, Roman and German worlds thus constitute the temporal-geographical trajectory of Spirit in world history. Thus in the introduction to *Philosophy of History*, Hegel begins with a critique of historical methodology to highlight its shortcomings. Then, on the ground of this critique, he argues that in virtue of the instrumental role of reason, philosophy is sensitive to the inherent continuity of historical events as the manifestation of providence. Lastly, Hegel asserts Spirit's unfolding as the basis of the universality of world history.

Sub-Saharan African Religious Practices and Vodou Cosmology

Hegel provides his analysis of the material context of world history in the section of *Philosophy of History* entitled "Geographical Basis of History". This section also contains Hegel's musings on Africa and the Americas. A notable aspect of Hegel's consideration of the material dimension of world history is that Spirit manifests itself through specific social, religious and cultural practices of a given people. Spirit encompasses the synthesis of the geographical context of a given people with their laws and customs. Hegel thinks that

> we began with the assertion that, in the History of the World, the Idea of Spirit appears in its actual embodiment as a series of external forms, each one of which declares itself as an actually existing people. This existence falls under the category of Time as well as space, in the way of natural existence; and the special principle, which every world-historical people embodies, has this principle at the same time as a natural characteristic.[10]

In claiming that Spirit's unfolding requires time, space and natural characteristics, Hegel is engaging in the Enlightenment practice of assigning national characteristics to peoples on the ground of their geographical context. Like Hume in his essay *Of National Characters* (1754) and Kant's *Observations on the Feelings of the Sublime and Beautiful* (1764), Hegel commits to the belief in uniformity between a people's national characteristic and their geographical environment. On the basis of this uniformity, Hegel asserts the Old and New Worlds as the legitimate geographical contexts of Spirit's unfolding.

The section "Geographical Basis of History" plays a central role in Hegel's *Lectures* because it bears his standpoint on European colonialism, the Americas and the cultural and religious practices of Africans. In this account, Hegel manages to strategically articulate his belief in European superiority and his view of Africans and people of African descent. In Hegel's mind:

> Negroes are enslaved by Europeans to be sold to America, bad as this may be, their lot in their own land is even worse, since there a slavery quite as absolute exists; for it is the essential principle of slavery, that man has not yet attained a consciousness of his freedom, and that consequently sinks down to a mere Thing – an object of no value. Among the Negroes moral sentiments are quite weak, or more strictly speaking non-existent.[11]

This statement aligns the enslavement of Africans with providential and logical necessity. It is noteworthy that Hegel crafts the first sentence of the above statement to surreptitiously link the epithet "Negroes", which refer to sub-Saharan Africans, with slavery. He then proceeds to imbue the epithet "Negroes" with its derogative connotations – namely, "an object of no value", "no consciousness of freedom" and "weak and non-existing moral sentiments". Bear in mind that at the time Hegel is delivering these lectures, he is regarded as the most important European philosopher, so in depicting

Africans under the epithet "Negroes" with derogative connotations, he is framing both the philosophical and larger European perception of Africans and people of African descent. Hegel's philosophical system invents the "Negroes" as both objects to be subjugated and receptacles of violence. This view of Africans, it will be shown in the following chapter, is equally espoused by Immanuel Kant in his *Science of Rights*.

Hegel's account justifies the slavery of Africans and the exclusion of Africa from being a historical period for God to reveal its being. In Hegel's mind, God simply does not reveal its being to Africans. Moreover, by situating his discussion of Africans in the section that pertains to the geographical and natural dimensions of world history, Hegel surreptitiously reduces enslaved Africans to the material basis of Spirit's unfolding. The latent premise of Hegel's argument is that Africans' lack of humanity justifies their enslavement. For Hegel, Africans' slavish disposition consists of their *thinghood*, which is confirmed by the absence of "moral sentiments". Hegel depicts enslaved Africans in the New World as mere natural and material entities without a specific role in universal history. In virtue of this standpoint, Hegel reinforces the philosophical and religious support that German Idealism and, more broadly, the Enlightenment provided to the transatlantic slave trade.

Hegel recognizes the United States as a sovereign nation of the New World, which is nevertheless inferior to the Old World. It is only worthy of recognition because: "what takes place in America is but an emanation from Europe".[12] America is an "emanation" of Europe because of similarities between their sociopolitical and religious institutions and because it is populated by people of European descent. For Hegel, America is a Eurocentric stronghold in the New World. Europe and European-colonized America were, he believed, history's dominant agent in "the modern time" justifying the colonizing project as the development of reason in the world.[13] Colonialism and slavery are thus logically and providentially necessary. In Hegel's mind, it is a manifestation of God's will that Africans are enslaved; its positive outcome consists in extricating Africans from their inherent barbarity.

Furthermore, Hegel believes that sub-Saharan Africans' religious practices and customs makes them opaque to European rationalization: "Africa must be divided into three parts: one is that which lies south of the desert of Sahara – Africa proper – the upland almost entirely unknown to us, with narrow coast-tracts along the sea; the second is that to the north of the desert – European Africa (if we may so call it) – a coastland; the third is the river region of the Nile, the only valley-land of Africa, and which is in connection with Asia."[14] This characterization of the part of Africa south of the desert of Sahara as "Africa proper" implies that his account of the African character focuses on Africans of this region. Hegel's discussion excludes the northern part of Africa and the river region of the Nile due to the former's espousal of European practices and the latter's contiguity to Asia. Unlike sub-Saharan Africans, whose character Hegel deems "peculiar", North Africans' and Asians' national characters are transparent to European rationalization because of their congeniality to European customs. The claim that sub-Saharan Africa is "unknown to us" defines the blackness of sub-Saharan Africans; their blackness consists in their opaqueness to "us", the Europeans. Hegel's claim reinforces the alterity of Africans as the black, opaque and inferior other of the European.

However, Hegel's account of Africans is conflicting. There is a contradiction in Hegel's preluding his account with the assertion that "The peculiarly African character is difficult to comprehend", which asserts their opaqueness to European rationalization, and then proceeding to provide a nine-page long elaboration of the character of Africans. Why does Hegel bother to provide an account of the peculiar and difficult character of Africans? The answer is that in describing the character of Africans, Hegel is justifying their exclusion from universal history and inventing "the Negroes". He wants to show that Africans as "peculiar" and "difficult to comprehend" lies beyond the grasp of European universality. For Hegel, consequently, sub-Saharan Africans are mere material particulars which fall outside the purview of his Protestant-centred universality.

Given that sub-Saharan Africans' cultural and social practices are opaque to European rationalization, Hegel shifts his focus to their religious rituals instead. Since Africans resist philosophical comprehension, he then draws from their religious rituals to emphasize the absence of meaningful social organization among them. Hegel provides a religious depiction of sub-Saharan Africans in the following:

> The peculiarly African character is difficult to comprehend, for the very reason that in reference to it we must give up the principle which naturally accompanies all our ideas – the category of universality. In Negro life the characteristic point is the fact that consciousness has not yet attained to the realization of any substantial objective existence – as for example, God, or Law – in which the interest of man's volition is involved and in in which he realizes his own being. This distinction between himself as an individual and the universality of his essential being, the African in the uniform, undeveloped oneness of his existence has not yet attained; so that the Knowledge of an absolute Being, an Other and a Higher than his individual self, is entirely wanting.[15]

It is noteworthy that Hegel attributes the Africans' peculiar character to the lack of a consciousness of God and law. Hegel's emphasis upon "our ideas" suggests that the character of Africans essentially eludes his Protestant philosophical idealism. By God and law, Hegel means the Christian godhead and European mores. Hegel was a profoundly religious philosopher. And what Hegel describes may in fact be a peculiarly European mind, and a nineteenth-century mind at that.[16] The above claim suggests that Hegel's Protestantism was near obscurantism. Moreover, the statement above suggests that for Hegel, Africans are inherently antisocial and lawless entities who are fully immersed in their natural environment. This characterization of Africans is in tune with his belief that Africans are only fit to supply the material basis of the Spirit's unfolding; Africans are fit to provide the material production necessary for the development of universal history; they are natural colonial commodities.

Another illustration of Hegel's Protestant philosophical take on Africa is in his account of the cultural practices of Africans, a trait he links to their religious disposition. For Hegel, religion trumps culture among Africans. The African individual is a material and religious entity and that is why

> the grade of culture which the Negroes occupy may be more nearly appreciated by considering the aspect which Religion presents among them. That which forms the basis of religious conceptions is the consciousness of man of a Higher Power – even though this is conceived only as a *vis naturae* – in relation to which he feels himself a weaker, humbler being. Religion begins with the consciousness that there is something higher than man. But even Herodotus called the Negroes sorcerers: – now in Sorcery we have not the idea of a God, of a moral faith; it exhibits man as the highest power, regarding

him as alone occupying a position of command over the power of Nature. We have here therefore nothing to do with a spiritual adoration of God, nor with the empire of Right. God thunders, but is not on that account recognizes as God. For the soul of man God must be more than a thunderer, whereas among the Negroes this is not the case. Although they are necessarily conscious of dependence upon nature – for they need the beneficial influence of storm, rain, cessation of the rainy period, and so on – yet this does not conduct them to the consciousness of a Higher Power: it is they who command the elements and this they call "magic". The Kings have a class of ministers through whom they command elemental changes and every place possesses such magicians, who perform special ceremonies with all sorts of gesticulations, dances, uproar, and shouting, and in the midst of this confusion commence their incantations.[17]

Hegel asserts the lack of consciousness of a Higher Power among sub-Saharan Africans by conflating their cultural practices with their religious rituals. According to Hegel's depiction, sub-Saharan Africans are mere idolaters because there is no Godhead as the object of their rituals. In defining these rituals as magic, Hegel implies that Africans idolize natural artefacts: "The religion of magic – the first religion, the form of nature religion, is the crudest and simplest. This is what we can call the religion of magic, the oldest, rawest, crudest form of religion."[18] Hence, Africans' religious reality amounts merely to the idolatry of natural artefacts. Thus, when viewed from Hegel's Protestantism, sub-Saharan Africans' religious consciousness is indeed mere idolatry.

Haitian Vodou and Sub-Saharan Religious Rituals

However, unbeknownst to Hegel, his rendition of the sub-Saharan Africans' religious rituals provides a description of the rituals of Vodun – the original system of African religious rituals and beliefs which were practised and held in various parts of southern sub-Sahara. Vodun consists of the plurality of African religious realities throughout Africa, which were practised as Vodou in Saint-Domingue. Hegel's portrayal of Africans' religious practices and beliefs suggests their similarity to Vodou practices in Saint-Domingue. In Haitian Vodou, it is common practice for farmers to beg for successful harvest from the lwas. Moreover, what Hegel refers to as "magic" illustrates

Vodou adherents' belief that the lwas and their ancestors are able to influence natural elements in their favour, especially for good harvests. Lastly, Hegel's description is loyal to the organization of Vodou rituals because the group of ministers that "the Kings" call upon to fulfil their requests match the function of the houngans (Vodou priests). The "uproar", "shouting", "dances" and "singing" that Hegel mentions above are typical practices in Vodou rituals. Also, Hegel's further elaboration of the "genius" below is evocative of the lwas in Vodou:

> The second element in their religion consists in their giving an outward form to this supernatural power – projecting their hidden might into the world of phenomena by means of images. What they conceive of as the power in question is therefore nothing really objective, having a substantial being and different from themselves, but the first thing that comes in their way. This, taken quite indiscriminately, they exalt to the power of a "Genius"; it may be an animal, a tree, a stone, or a wooden figure.[19]

Like Hegel's "Genius", lwas are believed to be able to assume the appearance of a peasant, an animal or an image. Hence, Hegel's account of sub-Saharan Africans' rituals is consistent with the organization of Vodou rituals in Saint-Domingue and, later, Haiti. However, Hegel's Protestant biased philosophical constructs against Africans and African religious reality led him to overlook the coherence between the "Genius", the religious rituals and the ministers as religious constituents of a distinctive cosmology. As a Protestant obscurantist, his oversight of the inherent continuity of the rituals leads him to depict sub-Saharan Africans' rituals as chaotic and to deem their temperaments peculiar.

Buck-Morss's Conflation of Vodou and Freemasonry

In *Hegel, Haiti, and Universal History* (2009), Buck-Morss is sensitive to the inherent continuity of Vodou practices in observing that the rise of Vodou in Saint-Domingue falls under "Atlantic Cosmologies". In contrast to Hegel, Buck-Morss is cognizant that Vodou in Saint-Domingue falls under a non-Western cosmology. Also, Buck-Morss's view of the configuration of Vodou in Saint-Domingue is sensitive to the context of the slave trade. Haitian

Vodou cosmology falls under Buck-Morss's "Atlantic Cosmologies" in rising as a by-product of the transatlantic slave trade during the Enlightenment.

However, her account is hindered by a key limitation: it reduces Vodou in Saint-Domingue to practices of Freemasonry in slave communities. Following Alfred Métraux, Buck-Morss states: "'Has Freemasonry contributed its share to the ceremony of Vodou? So it is said' writes the anthropologist Alfred Métraux in his study of the Haitian religious cult. Vodou has changed over time and its relation to Haitian Freemasonry. But contemporaries of the Age of Revolution perceived Vodou as 'a sort of religious and dancing masonry' with reason, given its embrace of strangers and syncretic epistemology."[20]

In reducing Vodou to a dancing and religious form of Freemasonry, Buck-Morss neglects the distinctive synthesis of various African religious practices inherent to Haitian Vodou. The issue is that this account portrays Haitian Vodou as an extension of Freemasonry practices on the plantations of Saint-Domingue which monkishly reproduces the plantation owners' secret rituals. Buck-Morss's depiction of Vodou as the medium of trustful bonds among disparate slaves is accurate: "It was the shared trauma of defeat, slavery, banishment, and the horrors of the Atlantic crossing and plantation labor that Vodou, in a burst of cultural creation, transformed into a community of trust."[21] Buck-Morss articulates the social and ethical import of Vodou to slave communities in Saint-Domingue; it is apt to guide the slaves of Saint-Domingue in the elaboration of a distinct national identity. Buck-Morss's account transcends the short-sighted account of Vodou as a mere African form of spirituality and asserts its role in shaping social attitudes. However, Buck-Morss fails to appreciate the cosmological discontinuity between Vodou, an African-based cosmology, and Freemasonry, a Western-based cosmology, in grounding their similarity in the fact that they both share secrecy. "Vodou was public religion as well as a secret society. Like Freemasonry, given the need to communicate visually when common language was lacking, emblems, secret signs, mimetic performance, and ritual were fundamental. And like Freemasonry, shared knowledge was envisioned as an amalgam of elements drawn from a whole variety of human cultures, open and additive, rather than hierarchically closed."[22]

Even though Buck-Morss is accurate that Freemasonry and Vodou share secrecy and are inclusive in nature, her comparison overlooks the historical circumstances of their rise and the Western inheritance of Freemasonry in contradistinction to Vodou. Secrecy was indeed an essential dimension of Vodou in Saint-Domingue as a mechanism of resistance to slavery. However, Freemasonry's secrecy preserves religious secrets of elite groups. The fact that Freemasonry, unlike Vodou practices, did not have to worry about annihilation from the slave masters acting on behalf of the edicts of *Le Code Noir* makes the secrecy of Vodou and Freemasonry different in scope and purpose. Buck-Morss's comparison is intended to make Vodou accessible and transparent to Westerners; however, this comparison downplays the radical orientation of Vodou cosmology as essentially an African-based cosmology with a different orientation and purpose. Buck-Morss then uses the analogy between Vodou and Freemasonry to reflect on the position of Haiti in universal history and modernity. Buck-Morss states:

> The rightful source of Haitian religious practice is the experience of slavery, leading to the insurrection of 1791. The rightful source of universal history, however, is not in the specifically Haitian articulation of that event – even less in its absorption by narratives of the French Revolution. Universality is in the moment of the slaves' self-awareness that the situation was not humanly tolerable, that it marked the betrayal of civilization and the limits of cultural understanding, the nonrational, the nonrationalizable course of human history that outstrips in its inhumanity anything that a cultural outlaw could devise.[23]

Buck-Morss's argument that the Haitian Revolution belongs in universal history is concomitant to the analogy of Vodou to Freemasonry. Viewing Haitian Vodou and Freemasonry as analogues downplays the African heritage of the former while ensuring that, in contrast to Hegel's denial, both the Haitian Revolution and a sovereign Haiti belong to universal history.

The Misrecognition of the Haitian Revolution in Hegel's Absolute Idealism

Hegel's remarks below about the absence of respect for life among Africans as the justification for them "to be shot down by thousands in war with Europeans" suggests an implicit reference to the Haitian Revolution: "To this want of regard for life must be ascribed the great courage, supported by enormous bodily strength, exhibited by the Negroes who allowed themselves to be shot down by thousands in war with Europeans. Life has a value only when it has something valuable as its object."²⁴

Hegel delivered the lectures of *Philosophy of History* during 1822–23 and 1830–32, almost twenty to thirty years after the end of the Haitian Revolution in 1804. Even though there were several conflicts in which Africans were massacred by Europeans in Africa and the New World's colonies, the fact that Hegel states a "war" instead of wars makes it plausible that he had in mind the Haitian Revolution in which thousands of Saint-Domingue's slaves died fighting Napoleon's army. In this passage, Hegel chooses not to acknowledge the Haitian Revolution explicitly and downplays the valour of the slaves to an "insignificant sacrifice", given that he previously depicts Africans in his account of sub-Saharan Africans as lacking the "higher purpose" which would make the act of dying for freedom a valorous act. If we accept the above passage as an implicit allusion to the Haitian Revolution, then Buck-Morss's contention that Hegel does not discuss the Haitian Revolution in the *Phenomenology of Spirit* because of dire financial and social circumstances becomes questionable. In Buck-Morss's words:

> In the Jena years, Hegel was feeling anything but the great figure we now take him to be. When he completed the Phenomenology, he was only thirty-six, and his life was in shambles. Terry Pinkard's recent biography describes Hegel's existential destitution: "With no money, no real paying job, and a child by a woman who was married to someone who had recently abandoned her [Hegel's landlord!], Hegel's situation now became completely and totally desperate." Such a man was not likely to include in his first major publication explicit references to Haiti that would be appreciated by neither the German authorities, nor Napoleon who was responsible for Toussaint L'Ouverture's recent death and was just then invading Hegel's city.²⁵

If Buck-Morss is indeed accurate that Hegel had no other motive besides financial duress and fear of reprisals for not discussing the Haitian Revolution explicitly in the *Phenomenology*, he could have discussed the Haitian Revolution in the introduction to *Philosophy of History*. Instead, he dismisses it a second time, despite the fact that when delivering these lectures, he was financially comfortable and renowned as the most important European philosopher.

Hegel finally makes explicit reference to Haiti in the lectures manuscript of *Philosophy of Mind* (1830, 1845). This tardy discussion reveals the centrality of Haiti in Hegelian thought. In his acknowledgement, he reluctantly recognizes Haiti under the aegis of a Christian nation. For him, it is undeniable that

> Negroes are to be regarded as a race of children who remain immersed in their state of uninterested *naïveté*. They are sold, and let themselves be sold, without any reflection on the rights or wrongs of the matter. The Higher which they feel they do not hold fast to, it is only a fugitive thought. This Higher they transfer to the first stone they come across, thus making it their fetish and they throw this fetish away if it fails to help them. Good natured and harmless when at peace, they can become suddenly enraged and then commit the most frightful cruelties. They cannot be denied a capacity for education; not only have they, here and there, adopted Christianity with the greatest gratitude and spoken movingly of the freedom they have acquired through Christianity after a long spiritual servitude, but in Haiti they have even formed a State on Christian principles.[26]

Indeed, the explicit reference to Haiti in Hegel's mature philosophy suggests that Saint-Domingue's revolution informed his dialectic of Lord and Bondsman and (perhaps most critically) presents his final view of Haiti. Hegel's characterization of Haiti as "a State on Christian principles" in *Philosophy of Mind* is consistent with his Protestant philosophically biased reading of sub-Saharan Africans' religious rituals in the introduction to *Philosophy of History*. In Hegel's mind, Christianity rids the Haitian people of the derogatory characteristics he assigns to Africans; it is proof that Christianity is fit to assist Africans in overcoming their opaqueness to European rationalization. In Hegel's mind, Christianity makes Africans less "Negroes". The underlying incentive of Hegel's recognition of Haiti as a Christian state is that Christianity neutralizes the inherent tyranny, cannibalism and lack of self-reverence he ascribes to the Africans of Saint-Domingue. Being able to adopt Christianity is, for Hegel, the evidence that Africans are indeed fit to transcend their inherent barbaric condition and opaqueness to European rationalization. In Hegel's philosophical system, rational transparency in world history depends on a people's fitness to espouse European and Christian mores. Hegel's recognition of Haiti is both religiously laden and biased because it overlooks Haiti's African heritage and the import of

Vodou cosmology to their social and ethical attitudes. Also, characterizing Haiti as a Christian state assigns both the Saint-Domingue revolution and Haiti a suitable conceptual space in his absolute idealism; Haiti becomes a premise in the logical unfolding of Spirit as a Christian nation. Hegel's take on Haiti suggests his conviction in Christianity's civilizing virtues; it assures homogeneity between Enlightened Europe and Haiti. The following section takes up Kant's explicit take on slavery and African slaves to show how the Enlightenment's perspective on Africans shaped the European reception of the Haitian Revolution.

CHAPTER 4.

Vodou Cosmology as Methodology of the Haitian Revolution

The argument of this chapter is that Vodou cosmology granted the slave communities of Saint-Domingue the religious unity, language and achievement of a common destiny as the requisites of state formation and the conviction of universal humanity that made the Haitian Revolution a successful critique and expansion of the Enlightenment's ideals. To make this argument, I show that overcoming tribal differences and the intersection of Vodou practices and marronage in Saint-Domingue contributed to the elaboration of a shared national identity. I borrow Neil Roberts's paradigm, which says:

> Marronage (marronage, maroonage, maronage) conventionally refers to a group of persons isolating themselves from a surrounding society in order to create a fully autonomous community, and for centuries it has been integral to interpreting the idea of freedom in Haiti as well as other Caribbean islands and Latin American countries including the Dominican Republic, Jamaica, Suriname, Venezuela, Brazil, Cuba, Colombia, and Mexico. These communities of freedom – known variously as "maroon societies", *quilombos, palenques, mocambos, cumbes, mambises, Rancherias, ladeiras, magotes, and manieles* – geographically situate themselves from areas slightly outside the borders of a plantation to the highest mountains of a region located as a far away from plantation life as possible.[1]

Also, given that I am arguing that the Haitian Revolution was a critique of the Enlightenment ideals of freedom and that it expands the prevailing Enlightenment view of freedom by extending it to the slaves of Saint-Domingue, I provide a discussion of Kant's essay *What is Enlightenment?* (1784) and his outlook on slavery and African peoples as colonial commodities in his *The*

Science of Right (1790) to show that Kant's ideals of the Enlightenment were European male–centred and presupposed freedom from forced labour to be fulfilled. These ideals assert European humanity in contradistinction to slaves as colonial commodities. To further the critique of the Enlightenment's ideals, I engage with Michel Rolph-Trouillot's critique of the Enlightenment to prove that his view that the Haitian Revolution was unthinkable from the perspective of the leaders and slaves of Saint-Domingue is the implication of his implicit espousal of the Enlightenment's depiction of African slaves. It concludes that religious unity, language and the achievement of a common destiny, which derive from Vodou cosmology, made the Haitian Revolution a cohesive and strategic historical event.

The Haitian Revolution and the Boundaries of European Enlightenment

Kant's essay *What Is Enlightenment?* unfolds judiciously on the basis and limits of the Enlightenment while asserting indirectly the end of medieval tyranny on European cultural, social and political practices. His definition is that "Enlightenment is man's release from his self-incurred tutelage. Tutelage is man's inability to make use of his understanding without direction from another. Self-incurred is this tutelage when its cause lies not in lack of reason but in lack of resolution and courage to use it without direction from another.... For this enlightenment, however, nothing is required but freedom, and indeed the most harmless among all the things to which this term can properly be applied. It is the freedom to make public use of one's reason at every point."[2]

The fact that Kant only posits rational freedom suggests that he takes the physical freedom of his audience as a given and that his discourse about the Enlightenment is not intended for slave communities. Freedom from tutelage and rational freedom are birthrights of Westerners. Kant is emphatic upon the Enlightenment's requirement to "use one's understanding without the direction from another". A legitimate question then is: who is this other? As Kant's essay unfolds it becomes obvious that he has in mind monarchy, organized religion and the monarchy's use of organized religion to justify their rule over the peoples of Europe. In Kant's words:

> I have placed the main point of Enlightenment – the escape of men from their self-incurred tutelage – chiefly in matters of religion because our rulers have no interest in playing the guardian with respect to the arts and sciences and also because religious immaturity is not only the most harmful but also the most degrading of all. But the manner of thinking of the head of a state who favors religious Enlightenment goes farther, and sees that there is no danger to his sovereignty in allowing his subjects to make public use of their reason and to publish their thoughts on better formulation of his legislation and even their open-minded criticisms of the laws already made.[3]

For Kant, only enlightened monarchies are suitable for the Enlightenment. Enlightened monarchies make their policies and the ground of their authority transparent to their subjects and do not hinder the progress and methodology of the arts and sciences. For Kant, religion may remain within the purview of the Enlightenment unless it is inner religion – the opposite of organized religion – which allows religious adherents the use of their faculties in matters of religious faith. Hence, Kant's discourse about the Enlightenment aims at securing the rational, aesthetic, religious and scientific autonomy of Westerners.

In *The Science of Right* (1790), Kant reflects on slavery in the context of the system of rights which justify the legitimacy of the state. Citizenship is inherently tied with rights and obedience to the laws of the state. For Kant, citizens are deemed free only within the confines of their rights and in obeying the state's laws. As an extension of this view, he believes that slavery is justified as a punishment for breaking the state's laws. In committing a crime, Kant thinks, criminals forsake their dignity and the rights that they enjoy as citizens of the state. In relinquishing one's rights, the previous citizen becomes a slave. Kant describes the transition from citizen of the state to slavery below:

> As a criminal he is still maintained in life, but he is made the mere instrument of the will of another, whether it be the state or a particular citizen. In the latter position, in which he could only be placed by a juridical judgement, he would practically become a slave, and would belong as property (dominium) to another, who would be not merely his master (herus) but his owner (dominus). Such an owner would be entitled to exchange or alienate him as a thing, to use him at will except for shameful purposes, and to dispose of his powers, but not of his life and members.[4]

The criminal, now slave, is a previous citizen who chose to become a tool; criminals forsake their citizenship's privileges. Kant emphasizes that a legal process is mandatory in order to carry out the transition of the criminal to slavery. The dignity of citizens requires a legal process in order to justify their slavery. Thus, in Kant's mind, slaves have both humanity and worthiness which protect them from being used for "shameful purposes and to dispose of their life and members".

This view of slavery differs radically from Kant's take on African slaves who, for him, have no humanity or legal standing. Kant lumps African peoples with colonial goods to be used according to the will of their owners and for commercial purpose. In *The Science of Right*, the discussion of African slaves is a corollary to Kant's argument about money as an indirect means to acquire goods. As such, African slaves are currency for commercial exchange among European powers and slave owners:

> But how is it possible that what at the beginning constituted only goods or wares, at length became money? This has happened wherever a sovereign as great and powerful consumer of a particular substance, which he at first used merely for the adornment and decoration of his servants and court, has enforced the tribute of his subjects in this kind of material. Thus it may have been gold, or silver, or copper, or a species of beautiful shells called cowries, or even a sort of mat called makutes, as in Congo; or ingots of iron, as in Senegal; or Negro slaves, as on the Guinea Coast. When the ruler of the country demanded such things as imposts, those whose labour had to be put in motion to procure them were also paid by means of them, according to certain regulations of commerce then established, as in a market or exchange.[5]

Kant's position suggests that in the mercantilism of the Enlightenment, African slaves stand as mere commercial means. They are currency for commercial transactions between the European metropolis and its colonies. Given Hegel's endorsement of African enslavement, previously discussed, as a providential event in the logical revelation of God's being and Kant's view of African slaves as commercial commodities, it is plain that in their ideals of the Enlightenment, the enslavement of Africans is necessary for the expansion of the European empire. Under the light of Kant and Hegel views of African slavery, the Haitian Anthropologist Rolph-Trouillot's castigation of Enlightenment philosophers is in order because it brings their inherent biases to the fore. Rolph-Trouillot summarizes his contention with the Enlightenment in the following passage:

> The West was created somewhere at the beginning of the sixteenth century in the midst of a global wave of material and symbolic transformations. What we call the Renaissance, much more an invention in its own right than a rebirth, ushered in a number of philosophical questions to which politicians, theologians, artists, and soldiers provided both concrete and abstract answers. What is beauty? What is Order? What is the State? But also above all: What is Man? Philosophers who discussed that last issue could not escape the fact that colonization was going on as they spoke.... Indeed, the slave trade increased in the years 1789–91 while French politicians and philosophers were debating more vehemently than ever on the rights of humanity.[6]

Rolph-Trouillot's observation exposes the limitations of the European Enlightenment. The intellectual projects that Rolph-Trouillot posits at the core of the Enlightenment map out a new regime of truths and the infrastructure of European sociopolitical organizations. His account is equally sensitive to the role played by slavery in the material transformation of Europe from medieval Europe into Imperial Europe. In Rolph-Trouillot's mind, Enlightenment philosophers such as Kant and Hegel were actively engaged in justifying imperial Europe and reducing African slaves to its material basis.

Also, Rolph-Trouillot's criticism draws out another dimension of the Enlightenment that is often overlooked. The Enlightenment is usually interpreted as a rupture with medieval religious tutelage and the fulfilment of the Renaissance scientific and rational standard. By relying on scientific standard, the aim was to grant European peoples rational and social autonomy. However, Rolph-Trouillot's assessment makes it apparent that the proponents of the Enlightenment define European humanity in contradistinction to the inhumanity of slaves in the colonies. Essentially, part of the answer to the Enlightenment's question of "What is man?" depends on the implicit assertion of the inhumanity of slaves and their inability to self-determine.

Rolph-Trouillot proceeds on the premise of the exclusion of African slaves from the Enlightenment's ideal of humanity to observe that the Haitian Revolution could not have been conceived by Europeans. In Rolph-Trouillot's words:

> To sum up in spite of the philosophical debates, in spite of the rise of abolitionism, the Haitian revolution was unthinkable in the West not only because it challenged slavery and racism but because of the way it did so.... The Haitian revolution was the ultimate test to the universalist pretensions of both the French and the American revolutions. And they both failed. In 1791, there is no public debate on the record, in France, in England, or in the United States on the right of black slaves to achieve self-determination, and the right to do so by way of armed resistance.[7]

Rolph-Trouillot asserts the unthinkability of the Haitian Revolution by Europeans on the Enlightenment's premise that only Europeans, as rational entities, are fit to carry out strategic revolutions. And since slaves are arational commodities, they are naturally unfit to undertake strategic revolutions. The unthinkability of the Haitian Revolution is consistent with the epistemological frame of the Enlightenment. In excluding the slaves of Saint-Domingue from the category of humanity and rational entities, the Enlightenment's conceptual apparatus could not have conceived the rise of a planned revolution from their midst.

However, Rolph-Trouillot's critique of the Enlightenment becomes problematic in claiming that the Haitian Revolution was equally unthinkable from the perspective of the slaves of Saint-Domingue and their leaders. Rolph-Trouillot thinks that

> not only was the Revolution unthinkable and, therefore, unannounced in the West, it was also – to a large extent – unspoken among the slaves themselves. By this I mean that the revolution was not preceded or even accompanied by an explicit intellectual discourse. One reason is that most slaves were illiterate and the printed word was not a realistic means of propaganda in the context of a slave colony. But another reason is that the claims of the revolution were indeed too radical to be formulated in advance of its deeds. Victorious practice could assert them only after the fact. In that sense, the revolution was indeed at the limits of the thinkable, even in Saint-Domingue, even among the slaves, even among its own leaders.... Toussaint himself may have not believed in the possibility of independence whereas, for all practical purposes, he was ruling Saint-Domingue as if it were independent.[8]

Rolph-Trouillot deems intellectual discourse and literacy as the sole media for revolutionary organization. In this view, the slave communities of Saint-Domingue are naturally arational and unfit for such coherent organization. For Rolph-Trouillot, given that slaves were illiterate, they are unfit to plan a strategic revolt; the Haitian Revolution was consequently sheer spontaneity. Its coherent unfolding could only be deduced *a posteriori* after its occurrence. His denial of the slaves' and their leaders' fitness to plan the Haitian Revolution provides a moderate reiteration of Kant and Hegel view of African slaves as thoughtless commodities. Thus, in espousing the unfitness of the slave communities and their leaders to plan a strategic revolution, Rolph-Trouillot inadvertently succumbs to the limitations of the Enlightenment practices that he is critiquing in claiming that the Haitian Revolution could have been thinkable by the slaves and leaders unless they were able to perform intellectual discourse. As such, Rolph-Trouillot's argument surreptitiously inherits the Enlightenment's depiction of African slaves as unfit for intellectual discourse.

The Haitian Revolution as the Outcome of Vodou Cosmology

Moreover, Rolph-Trouillot's argument leaves us bereft of any coherent rendition of the unfolding of the Haitian Revolution as a process from the perspective of the leaders and fighters. If we accept Rolph-Trouillot's view of the occurrence of the Haitian Revolution as sheer spontaneity, then the Haitian Revolution is reduced to a mere historical coincidence. In what follows, I set out to argue that Vodou cosmology provided the requisite religious unity, language, achievement of common destiny as an axiom of state formation and the conviction of universal humanity that made the Haitian Revolution coherent with the circumstances of the fighters and leaders. I also argue that these achievements made the Haitian Revolution a strategic set of events from the perspective of the fighters and leaders.

Vodou rituals provided a language and medium to assist the social and religious assimilation of disparate slaves in Saint-Domingue. It depended on the collective memory of slaves, their shared ability to preserve and perpetuate African-based religious traditions. It was the focus for the development of political consciousness so far as it allowed the slaves to be aware that their values were different from those of the whites and also as far as it allowed them to express their negritude.[9] Of course, these traditions were not necessarily common. The disruption of the slave trade often placed, side by side, slaves from different regions, tribes, languages and beliefs. Accordingly, to simply transplant African practices was impossible. Vodou cosmology embodies essentially the religious negotiation of various tribal communities in establishing common ancestral basis to define their religious and social identity in Saint-Domingue. The slaves retained elements of the culture which they had known in Africa, in particular the Vodou religion, which was widely practised in the plantations. It was an amalgam of the various religious beliefs and practices of West Africa, which even incorporated certain Christian symbols.[10] Herein lies the collective and syncretistic nature of Vodou as both a system of religious practices and means for social cohesion. The traditional religions of Africa could hardly be perpetuated in toto in the New World because of the vast ecological differences between the continents.[11] And yet, despite the challenges of geographical and tribal differences, the displaced slaves in the Catholic regime managed to invent the suitable rituals to preserve their African-based cosmology. Neo-African cults, found in countries which are predominantly Catholic, have incorporated a considerable body of African traditions in their beliefs and rituals.[12]

Thus, the elaboration of Vodou cosmology is the by-product of a collective process to derive a common ethos and social orientation. In this way, it reflects Desquiron's description of Vodou as a "dual syncretism": "Le Vodou haïtien est le produit d'un double syncrétisme: le premier s'est accompli entre les différentes cultures africaines; le deuxième a eu lieu entre ces différentes cultures africaines et la culture occidentale."[13] (Haitian Vodou is the product of a dual syncretism: the first happened among the different African cultures; the second happened between these different African cultures and Western culture.) Indeed, Vodou unfolded simultaneously as the slaves established both the appropriate rituals and a socio-ethical map for self-orientation in a foreign environment under the harshness of slavery.

In this deeply alienating context, religion certainly provided an institution through which the African past of the slaves is preserved and also an instrument of solidarity and communication during the colonial period.[14] Finding common identity and social destiny was intrinsic to the practice of Vodou during slavery. Of course, as previously noted, the negotiation of rituals among slaves from different tribes brought with it considerable changes. Over and above these were the legal and religious restraints of *Le Code Noir* – a series of restrictions on the practice of any religion other than Roman Catholicism in the French colonies. Indeed, the secretive dimension of Vodou cosmology was indispensable to preserve it from the threat of extinction by *Le Code Noir*. The elaboration of Vodou as an African-based cosmology in Saint-Domingue thus displays slaves' ability to overcome the barriers of tribal difference as well as their resistance to this colonial mandate.

So, as a process, the elaboration of Vodou cosmology is characterized by collective negotiation of different tribal rituals in secret practices, which mapped out the creed of the new spirituality of the slaves. Thus, Vodou has to be characterized as a generic term, covering these various creolized cults.[15] It is unsurprising then that Vodou cosmology unfolds at the intersection of different rituals and deities which it simultaneously transcended and preserved. One of the sociopolitical implications of the process of overcoming tribal differences and formulating a common identity is that it compels the individual subjectivity of the practitioners to embrace the "we" as the marker of the collective, instead of the "I" as the classic marker of Western subjectivity. Slave communities' commitment to the "we" as the marker of an African-based subjectivity was the logical implication of syncretism and collective process inherent to Vodou cosmology. The rise of Vodou cosmology thus represents the successful attempt of isolated slave communities to reinvent the social and religious context of their original setting. Vodou was perhaps one of the most cohesive forces among the slaves and one which the whites tried to suppress.[16] Vodou cosmology is born out of the need for an existential praxis for self-orientation in the foreignness of Saint-Domingue by overcoming tribal differences and assimilating its norms. This process defines the social nature of Vodou cosmology. "Le vodou est créateur. D'une multitude d'hommes venus de toutes parts, d'ethnies bien différentes, voici que cette religion est en train d'en faire une société cohérente ... il transmet une institution qui conditionne l'efficacité de l'action à venir en vue d'une libération collective.[17] (Vodou is creative. From a large number of men who came from all parts, and different ethnicities, this religion is creating a coherent society. . . . It is the vehicle of an institution which conditions the effectiveness of the future act which leads to collective freedom.) Such collective negotiation defines the political and social potential of Vodou from its inception.

It is precisely in virtue of this social and collective nature that Vodou cosmology is conducive to the organization of the revolution that established Haiti as the first independent black nation. Indeed, the birth of Haiti and Haitian citizenship depended on several key factors rooted in the elaboration of Vodou cosmology. First, on the most general level, taking part in the activities of a cult or sect provides emotional support for members who are forced to live in a world that they often perceive as hostile, thereby allowing for the possibility of collective action.[18] Second, as discussed, Vodou provided disparate slaves with a sense of common sociopolitical destiny and confidence in their African-based national identity despite the legal and religious restrictions of *Le Code Noir* and slavery's eroding impact on individual subjectivity. Building socially coherent communities follows the same process which established Vodou cosmology. The initial manifestations of social cohesion that result from Vodou cosmology are the formation of Maroon communities. After all, the task of reconciliation among the slaves shipped to Saint-Domingue, hardly an issue of redistributing wealth, concerned building fraternal alliances of trust among former enemies of war and among persons massed together in labour gangs who had no common background and little understanding of each other. Indeed, they may not have known of each other's cultural existence before the crossing.[19]

Beginning in 1791, the Haitian Revolution stands as the culmination of marronage, secret organizations and frequent insurrections until the final war of 1804 led by Jean-Jacques Dessalines. Marronage is central to understanding the slaves' attempt to become free. It is the moment when the Maroon, a runaway slave, seeks freedom in the mountains. The Maroon-Vodou collaboration was pivotal at the outbreak of the Haitian Revolution, and Vodou became "the symbol of Haitian autonomy and nationalism as the only black republic in the Americas" in 1803. Boukman Dutty, a founder of the revolution, was a Maroon leader and Vodou priest, or papaloi, with an imposing physical stature. He was also known as Zamba.[20] Viewed from the perspective of the slave, the intersection of Maroon-Vodou suggests that the landscape of Saint-Domingue gradually lost its hostile and foreign aura.

Marronage assists the slave communities in systematically domesticating and appropriating Saint-Domingue.

Moreover, the occurrence of marronage articulates the shift of consciousness that occurred as the slaves started to perceive the mountain as a locus of freedom. It indicates the slaves' gradual ownership of Saint-Domingue as their homeland. Starting to view the mountains as free places within the colonial environment is linked to the secrecy of Vodou cosmology and the elaboration of a common language which articulates collective consciousness among the slaves. Given that the slaves were able to communicate the hiding places in the mountains to one another, there must have been a shared language as medium of communication. This is important because the elaboration of this common language is another indication of the slaves' transcendence of their tribal differences and their unity around an African-based semiotics, a meaningful system of words and signs as a shared medium of communication.

The rise of Creole in Saint-Domingue presupposes a system of signifiers and signified which articulates the grasp of both the physical and social dynamics of its speakers. Moreover, its role as one of the specifics of the Haitian Revolution is proof that the revolutionaries and leaders' possessed a systematic account of the revolutionary process. Haitian Creole, like other Creoles, developed as a "contact language", as did the "pidgin languages" spoken by motley crews. Its evolution is not well documented, given ignorance of linguistics generally until the twentieth century. Based primarily on French (just how close to the colonial planter class French it was is a matter of debate), it contains elements from Fon (as ethnolinguistic substratum), Ewe/Anlo-Ewe, Wolof and Gbe (all from the Niger region), as well as Bantu (from Kongo) and Arabic (via Islam).[21] As the linguistic brokering of these various tribal groups, the rise of Haitian Creole was feasible upon systematic and cooperative interactions among these groups. It is safe to believe that Haitian Creole was equally central in the secret planning of the revolution. Rolph-Trouillot's account is insensitive to the inherent systematicity of Haitian Creole and marronage. Marronage supplied the context and Haitian Creole provided the systematic means for the fighters and their leaders to plan the revolution.

The amalgamation of these various social and religious media in the slave communities is embodied in the figure of Boukman. Even though the particulars surrounding the planning of the slave rebellion are obscure, Boukman's role was certainly important. A huge, muscular man and a fugitive slave from Jamaica, Boukman was a Vodou priest who despised whites. He used the deep roots of Vodou among the slaves as a communications system to organize rebellion.[22] Boukman is probably the most interesting figure in the Haitian Revolution because his contribution synthesizes religion, systematic organization and collective trust in the process of the revolution. Boukman was fit to coordinate the Haitian Revolution on the continuity of these religious and social factors.

Moreover, the rise of Haitian Creole as a medium of communication shows the slaves' transcendence of the dissonance of slavery and the achievement of a shared medium of communication. Given that the hiding places were kept secret, the slaves must have learned to trust each other. Trust and secrecy are proof of social cohesion among the slaves. They demonstrate the recognition of shared social interests which must be kept from the masters' awareness. The frequent revolts and burning of plantations were linked to marronage because upon achieving confidence in the mountains as places of freedom, the next logical step was to attempt to expand them in the rest of the colony and make Saint-Domingue uniformly free. The slaves' proclivity to expand freedom through marronage and their perception of the mountain as a locus of freedom were incentives of the frequent revolts of the Haitian Revolution.

Of course, little is known about the slaves' discussions and exchanges while hiding in the mountains (emphasis is usually upon the final meeting, which occurred around the Vodou ceremony in Bois-Caiman). Such lack of literature may be the reason that prompted Rolph-Trouillot to believe that the Haitian Revolution was unthinkable even among the slaves and its leaders. However, it is undeniable that the Maroon communities were the predecessors of slave-based societies in the Caribbean. Maronnage provided the ideal theatre of freedom, community and social exchange among the slaves of Saint-Domingue prior to the rise of Haiti as a free nation. In learning to assume specific social roles in the Maroon community, the slaves develop social agency.

Accordingly, the Maroon transcends their slave consciousness as they learn to see themselves as an organizer with specific roles in the Maroon community. Social agency is concomitant to the secret organization of Maroon communities. It is an inherent dimension of citizenship because it maps out the roles that each participant ought to assume in order for the proper functioning of the sociopolitical institutions. Thus, a free Saint-Domingue was already latent in the Maroon communities, and the revolutionary process is best understood as the realization of this nascent independent consciousness.

The fact that a Vodou ceremony is believed to have been the prelude of the ultimate battle is consistent with both the rise of Vodou cosmology as the sociopolitical dimension of Vodou and the Maroons as the first free communities of Saint-Domingue. The ceremony celebrated the religious and sociopolitical confidence that Maroon communities achieved and the conviction that their freedom ought to pervade every aspect of the landscape. It is on such premise that the tripartite transition from slaves to Maroons and then to Haitian citizen occurs. The pioneering role of the Haitian Revolution is viewed accurately by Nesbitt as a radical Enlightenment. For Nesbitt, the rise of the Haitian state "announced that freedom can exist only when we create a global society whose structures and laws allow for the full and unimpeded development of our possibilities as living individuals. This pronouncement was shocking and inadmissible in a system of global colonialism grounded and dependent on the enslavement of a portion of the human population."[23] As a radical Enlightenment, the occurrence of the Haitian Revolution was both a major critique of the shortcoming of the European Enlightenment and the completion of its ideals. It exposed the inherent contradiction in positing freedom for humanity while excluding African peoples. Also, in granting freedom to the slaves of Saint-Domingue, it is the genuine fulfilment of the Enlightenment's belief that all human beings ought to be free from religious tutelage and forced labour.

In conclusion, the Haitian Revolution heralded the African Diaspora Enlightenment because it granted the slaves the consciousness of being of African descent and free, an idea that was anathema to the purview of Eurocentric ideals. It created the occasion for the slaves to overcome both physical and rational tutelage in consistency with Kant's requirement above. The tyranny of the monarchy and organized religion that Kant repudiates is the equivalent of the colonialist regime and the justification of slavery by the edicts of *Le Code Noir* in the French colonies. Through the occurrence of the Haitian Revolution, people of African descent became free social agents and the centre of their sociopolitical context. Furthermore, the occurrence of the Haitian Revolution undertakes a paradoxical shift of the Enlightenment. It displaces its conceptual purview in showing that reason, the central lynchpin of the Enlightenment, prevailed in slave communities. It allowed the slaves to secure the recognition of the West, as both humans and *res cogitans* – entities that are fit to reason and behave as sociopolitical agents. This recognition is articulated in the emergence of Saint-Domingue as the Republic of Haiti, the first black nation. Thus, the news of the Haitian Revolution was subversive among other slave communities because it triggered the consciousness of the possibility of being of African descent and free, which is synthesized in blackness, black power and black cultural expressions.

Notes

Introduction

1. Neil Roberts, *Freedom as Maronnage* (Chicago: University of Chicago Press, 2015), 5.

Chapter 1

1. Matthew J. Smith, *Red and Black in Haiti: Radicalism, Conflict, and Political Change, 1934–1957* (Chapel Hill: University of North Carolina Press, 2009), 58.
2. Maya Deren, *Divine Horsemen: The Living Gods of Haiti* (New Paltz, NY: McPherson, 1985), 59.
3. André Droogers and Sidney M. Greenfield, "Recovering and Reconstructing Syncretism", in *Reinventing Religions: Syncretism and Transformation in Africa and the Americas*, ed. Sidney M. Greenfield and André Droogers (Lanham, MD: Rowman and Littlefield, 2001), 24–25.
4. Lilas Desquiron, *Racines du Vodou* (Port-au-Prince: Éditions Henri Deschamps, 1990), 76.
5. Mozella Mitchell, *Crucial Issues in Caribbean Religion* (New York: Peter Lang, 2006), 65.
6. Deren, *Divine Horsemen*, 192.
7. Joan Dayan, "Vodoun or the Voice of the Gods", in *Sacred Possessions: Vodou, Santeria, Obeah, and the Caribbean*, ed. Margarite F. Olmos and Lizabeth Paravisini-Gebert (New Brunswick, NJ: Rutgers University Press, 2000), 18.
8. Michel S. Laguerre, *Voodoo and Politics in Haiti* (New York: St Martin's Press, 1989), 70.
9. David Nicholls, *From Dessalines to Duvalier: Race, Colour, and National Independence in Haiti* (New Brunswick, NJ: Rutgers University Press, 1996), 23.
10. Gérad A. Frère, "Haitian Voodoo: Its True Face", *Caribbean Quarterly* 24, nos. 3–4 (1978): 45; my emphasis.
11. Laguerre, *Voodoo and Politics*, 23.

12. George E. Simpson, *Black Religions in the New World* (New York: Columbia University Press, 1978), 14.
13. Desquiron, *Racines du Vodou*, 35.
14. Nicholls, *From Dessalines to Duvalier*, 31.
15. Frère, "Haitian Voodoo", 38.
16. Laguerre, *Voodoo and Politics*, 38.
17. Thomas Ott, *The Haitian Revolution* (Knoxville: University of Tennessee Press, 1973), 15.
18. Simpson, *Black Religions*, 17.
19. Susan Buck-Morss, *Hegel, Haiti, and Universal History* (Pittsburgh: University of Pittsburgh Press, 2009), 131–32.
20. Marie-José Alcide, "Theatrical and Dramatic Elements of Haitian Voodoo" (PhD diss., City University of New York, 1988), 62.
21. Laurent Dubois, *Haiti: The Aftershocks of History* (New York: Metropolitan Books, 2012), 107–11.
22. G.W.F. Hegel, *Phenomenology of Spirit,* trans. A.V. Miller (Oxford: Oxford University Press, 1977), 118–19.
23. Gillian Rose, *Hegel Contra Sociology* (London: Verso, 2009), 70.
24. C.L.R. James, *The Black Jacobins: Toussaint L'Ouverture and the San Domingo Revolution* (New York: Vintage, 1989), 85–86.
25. Zora Neale Hurston, *Tell My Horse: Voodoo and Life in Haiti and Jamaica* (New York: Harper and Row, 1990), 115–16.
26. Francis Huxley, *The Invisibles: Voodoo Gods in Haiti* (New York: McGraw-Hill, 1966), 204.
27. Ibid., 290–91.
28. M. Jacqui Alexander, *Pedagogies of Crossing: Meditations on Feminism, Sexual Politics, Memory, and the Sacred* (Durham, NC: Duke University Press, 2005), 301.
29. Deren, *Divine Horsemen*, 61.
30. Anthony Pinn, *Varieties of African-American Religious Experience* (Edinburgh: Augsburg Fortress Press, 1998), 24.
31. Ibid.
32. Rodolphe Derose, *Caractère, Culture Vodou: formation et interpretation de l'individualité haitienne* (Port-au-Prince: Bibliothèque haitienne, 1955), 123.
33. Smith, *Red and Black*, 48.
34. Laurent Dubois, *Avengers of the New World: The Story of the Haitian Revolution* (Cambridge, MA: Harvard University Press, 2004), 43.
35. Mary A. Renda, *Taking Haiti: Military Occupation and the Culture of U.S.*

Imperialism, 1915–1940 (Chapel Hill: University of North Carolina Press, 2001), 45.
36. Jean Joseph Jean, *God in the Haitian Voodoo Religion* (Pittsburgh: Dorrance, 2004), 27.
37. Hurston, *Tell My Horse*, 114.
38. Margarite Olmos and Lizabeth Paravisini-Gebert, "Introduction: Religious Syncrestism and Caribbean Culture", in *Sacred Possessions: Vodou, Santeria, Obeah, and the Caribbean*, ed. Margarite Olmos and Lizabeth Paravisini-Gebert (New Brunswick, NJ: Rutgers University Press, 1997), 4.
39. Karen McCarthy Brown, "Afro-Caribbean Spirituality: A Haitian Case Study", in *Vodou in Haitian Life and Culture: Invisible Powers*, ed. Claudine Michel and Patrick Bellegarde-Smith (New York: Palgrave Macmillan, 2006), 18.
40. Frère, "Haitian Voodoo", 41.
41. Olmos and Paravisini-Gebert, "Introduction", 21.
42. Ibid.
43. Jean Fils-Aimé, *Vodou, je me souviens: le combat d'une cultiure pour sa survie* (Montreal: Éditions Dabar, 2007), 101.
44. Olmos and Paravisini-Gebert, "Introduction", 28.

Chapter 2

1. Otfried Hoffe, *Immanuel Kant*, trans. Marshal Farrier (Albany: State University of New York Press, 1994), 159.
2. Immanuel Kant, *Groundwork of the Metaphysics of Morals*, trans. Lewis White Beck as *Foundations of the Metaphysics of Morals* (Trenton, NJ: Library of Liberal Arts, 1959), 17.
3. Immanuel Kant, *Critique of Practical Reason*, trans. Mary Gregor (Cambridge: Cambridge University Press, 1997), 26.
4. Christine Korsgaard, *Creating the Kingdom of Ends* (Cambridge: Cambridge University Press, 1996), 11.
5. Robert B. Brandom, *Reason in Philosophy: Animating Ideas* (Cambridge, MA: Harvard University Press, 2009), 60.
6. Korsgaard, *Creating the Kingdom*, 13.
7. Kant, *Critique*, 28.
8. Kant, *Groundwork*, 67.
9. Kant, *Critique*, 32.
10. Ibid.

11. Kant, *Groundwork*, 66.
12. Ibid., 65.
13. Kant, *Critique*, 53.
14. Ibid., 63.
15. Brandom, *Reason in Philosophy*, 63.
16. Maurice Lemoine, *Bitter Sugar: Slaves Today in the Caribbean* (Chicago: Banner Press, 1985), 83.
17. Dayan, "Vodoun", 25.
18. Brandom, *Reason in Philosophy*, 59.
19. Wade Davis, *Passage of Darkness: The Ethnobiology of the Haitian Zombie* (Chapel Hill: University of North Carolina Press, 1988), 37–38.
20. Dayan, "Vodoun", 19.
21. Ibid.
22. James, *Black Jacobins*, 86.
23. Ama Mazama, "Lwa", in *Encyclopedia of African Religion,* ed. Molefi Kete Asante and Ama Mazama, vol. 1 (Los Angeles: Sage, 2009), 392.
24. Michel and Bellegarde-Smith, *Vodou in Haitian Life*, 18.
25. Kant, *Critique*, 53.
26. Gérard Alphonse Férère and Pascale Bécel, "Vodoun", in *Encyclopedia of the African Diaspora: Origins, Experiences, and Culture*, ed. Carole Boyce Davies, vol. 3 (Santa Barbara, CA: ABC-Clio, 2008), 963.
27. Davis, *Passage of Darkness*, 45.
28. Kant, *Critique*, 63.
29. Inger Sjørslev, "Possession and Syncretism: Spirits as Mediators in Modernity", in *Reinventing Religions: Syncretism and Transformation in Africa and the Americas*, ed. Sidney M. Greenfield and André Droogers (Lanham, MD: Rowman and Littlefield, 2001), 135.

Chapter 3

1. G.W.F. Hegel, *The Philosophy of History*, trans. J. Sibree (New York: Prometheus Books, 1991), 9.
2. Ibid., 9–10.
3. William Desmond, "Nietzsche and Hegel", in *Hegel, History, and Interpretation*, ed. Shaun Gallagher (Albany: State University of New York Press, 1997), 75.
4. Hegel, *Philosophy of History*, 14–15.
5. Buck-Morss, *Hegel, Haiti, and Universal* History, 115–16.

6. Michael Inwood, *A Commentary on Hegel's Philosophy of Mind* (Oxford: Oxford University Press, 2010), 18.
7. Burleigh Wilkins, *Hegel's Philosophy of History* (Ithaca: Cornell University Press, 1974), 48.
8. Hegel, *Philosophy of History*, 53
9. George O'Brien, *Hegel on Reason and History: A Contemporary Interpretation* (Chicago: University of Chicago Press, 1975), 53.
10. Hegel, *Philosophy of History*, 79.
11. Ibid., 96.
12. Ibid., 82.
13. Buck-Morss, *Hegel, Haiti, and Universal History*, 116.
14. Hegel, *Philosophy of History*, 91.
15. Ibid., 93.
16. Inwood, *Commentary*, 18, 26.
17. Hegel, *Philosophy of History*, 93–94.
18. G.W.F. Hegel, *Lectures on the Philosophy of Religion*, vol. 2, ed. Peter Hodgson; trans. R.F. Brown, P.C. Hodgson and J.M. Stewart (Berkeley: University of California Press, 1987), 272.
19. Hegel, *Philosophy of History*, 94.
20. Buck-Morss, *Hegel, Haiti, and Universal History*, 123–24.
21. Ibid., 126.
22. Ibid.
23. Ibid., 133.
24. Hegel, *Philosophy of History*, 96.
25. Buck-Morss, *Hegel, Haiti, and Universal History*, 19–20.
26. G.W.F. Hegel, *Philosophy of Mind*, trans. A.V. Miller (Oxford: Oxford University Press, 1971), 43–44.

Chapter 4

1. Roberts, *Freedom as Maronnage*, 5.
2. Immanuel Kant, *What Is Enlightenment?*, trans. Lewis White Beck (Trenton, NJ: Library of Liberal Arts, 1997), 83–84.
3. Ibid., 89.
4. Immanuel Kant, *The Science of Right* (New York: Simon and Schuster 2012), 96.
5. Ibid., 55.
6. Michel Rolph-Trouillot, "An Unthinkable History: The Haitian Revolution

as a Non-Event", in *Haitian History: New Perspectives*, ed. Alyssa Sepinwall (London: Routledge, 2013), 35–37.
7. Ibid., 40–41.
8. Ibid., 41, 44.
9. Laguerre, *Voodoo and Politics*, 70.
10. Nicholls, *From Dessalines to Duvalier*, 23.
11. Laguerre, *Voodoo and Politics*, 23.
12. Simpson, *Black Religions*, 14.
13. Desquiron, *Racines du Vodou*, 35.
14. Nicholls, *From Dessalines to Duvalier*, 31.
15. Laguerre, *Voodoo and Politics*, 38.
16. Ott, *Haitian Revolution*, 15.
17. Guérin Montilus, "Haïti: un cas témoin de la vivacité des religions africaines en Amérique et pourquoi", in *Vodun* (Paris: Présence Africaine, 1993), 181.
18. Simpson, *Black Religions*, 17.
19. Buck-Morss, *Hegel, Haiti, and Universal History*, 131–32.
20. Ibid., 63.
21. Ibid., 120.
22. Ott, *Haitian Revolution*, 47.
23. Nick Nesbitt, *Universal Emancipation: The Haitian Revolution and the Radical Enlightenment* (Charlottesville: University of Virginia Press, 2008), 11.

Bibliography

Adorno, Theodor W. *Hegel: Three Studies*. Translated by Shierry Weber Nicholsen. Cambridge, MA: Massachussetts Institute of Technology Press, 1993.

———. *Kant's Critique of Pure Reason*. Edited by Rolf Tiedemann. Translated by Rodeny Livingstone. Stanford: Stanford University Press, 1995.

Alcide, Marie-José. "Theatrical and Dramatic Elements of Haitian Voodoo". PhD dissertation, City University of New York, 1988.

Alexander, M. Jacqui. *Pedagogies of Crossing: Meditations on Feminism, Sexual Politics, Memory and the Sacred*. Durham, NC: Duke University Press, 2005.

Allison, Henry E. *Idealism and Freedom: Essays on Kant's Theoretical and Practical Philosophy*. Cambridge: Cambridge University Press, 1996.

———. *Kant's Transcendental Idealism: An Interpretation and Defense*. New Haven: Yale University Press, 2004.

Anderson-Gold, Sharon. *Unnecessary Evil: History and Moral Progress in the Philosophy of Immanuel Kant*. Albany: State University of New York Press, 2001.

Arendt, Hannah. *Lectures on Kant's Political Philosophy*. Edited by Ronald Beiner. Chicago: University of Chicago Press, 1992.

Barnett, Stuart. *Hegel after Derrida*. New York: Routledge, 1993.

Baron, Marcia W. *Kantian Ethics Almost without Apology*. Ithaca: Cornell University Press, 1995.

Bécel, Pascale, and Gérard Alphonse Férère. "Vodoun". In *Encyclopedia of the African Diaspora: Origins, Experiences and Culture*, vol. 3, edited by Carole Boyce Davies, 962–63. Santa Barbara, CA: ABC-Clio, 2008.

Beiser, Frederick C., ed. *The Cambridge Companion to Hegel*. Cambridge: Cambridge University Press, 1993.

———. *The Fate of Reason: German Philosophy from Kant to Fichte*. Cambridge, MA: Harvard University Press, 1987.

Beckford, James A., ed. *New Religious Movements and Rapid Social Change*. Los Angeles: Sage, 1991.

Bellegarde-Smith, Patrick, ed. *Fragments of Bone: Neo-African Religions in a New World*. Champaign: University of Illinois Press, 2005.

Bird, Graham, ed. *A Companion to Kant*. Oxford: Blackwell, 2006.

Bisnauth, Dale. *A History of Religions in the Caribbean*. Trenton, NJ: Africa World Press, 1996.
Brandom, Robert B. *Reason in Philosophy: Animating Ideas*. Cambridge: Harvard University Press, 2009.
Brook, Andrew. *Kant and the Mind*. Cambridge: Cambridge University Press, 1994.
Brown, Karen McCarthy. *Mama Lola: A Vodou Priestess in Brooklyn*. Berkeley: University of California Press, 2001.
Buck-Morss, Susan. *Hegel, Haiti, and Universal History*. Pittsburgh: University of Pittsburgh Press, 2009.
Case, Frederick I., and Patrick Taylor, eds. *The Encyclopedia of Caribbean Religions*. Champaign: University of Illinois Press, 2013.
Chadwick, Ruth F., ed. *Immanuel Kant: Critical Assessments*. New York: Routledge, 1992.
Chalybaeus, Heinrich Moritz. *Historical Development of Speculative Philosophy from Kant to Hegel*. Edinburgh: T. and T. Clark, 1854.
Cholbi, Michael. *Understanding Kant's Ethics*. Cambridge: Cambridge University Press, 2016.
Clarke, Peter B. *New Trends and Developments in African Religions*. Westport, CT: Greenwood, 1998.
Collins, Ardis B., Ed., *Hegel and the Modern World*. Albany: State University of New York Press, 1995.
Copeland, Kwame F. *The Afro-Blues Tradition: Glorious Child of the Africans*. Lincoln, NB: IUniverse, 2006.
Dallmayr, Fred Reinhard. *G.W.F. Hegel: Modernity and Political Thought*. Lanham, MD: Rowman and Littlefield, 2002.
Davis, Wade. *Passage of Darkness: The Ethnobiology of the Haitian Zombie*. Chapel Hill: University of North Carolina Press, 1988.
Dayan, Joan. "Vodoun or the Voice of the Gods". In *Sacred Possessions: Vodou, Santeria, Obeah, and the Caribbean*, edited by Margarite F. Olmos and Lizabeth Paravisini-Gebert, 13–36. New Brunswick, NJ: Rutgers University Press, 1997.
DeLaurentis, Allegra, and Jeffrey Edwards, eds. *The Bloomsbury Companion to Hegel*. New York: Bloomsbury Acdemic, 2013.
Deligiorgi, Katerina. *Kant and the Culture of Enlightenment*. Albany: State University of New York Press, 2005.
Deren, Maya. *Divine Horsemen: The Living Gods of Haiti*. New Paltz, NY: McPherson, 1985.
Derose, Rodolphe. *Caractère, Culture Vodou: formation et interpretation de l'individualité haitienne*. Port-au-Prince: Bibliothèque haitienne, 1955.

Desmond, William. "Nietzsche and Hegel". In *Hegel, History, and Interpretation*, edited by Shaun Gallagher, 71–96. Albany: State University of New York Press, 1997.

Desquiron, Lilas. *Racines du Vodou*. Port-au-Prince: Éditions Henri Deschamps, 1990.

Detorre, Miguel A. *Santeria: The Beliefs and Rituals of a Growing Religion in America*. Grand Rapids, MI: Eerdmans, 2004.

Dorsey, Lilith. *Voodoo and Afro-Caribbean Paganism*. New York: Citadel, 2005.

Droogers, André, and Sidney M. Greenfield. "Recovering and Reconstructing Syncretism". In *Reinventing Religions: Syncretism and Transformation in Africa and the Americas*, edited by André Droogers and Sidney M. Greenfield, 21–42. Lanham, MD: Rowman and Littlefield, 2001.

Dubois, Laurent. *Avengers of the New World: The Story of the Haitian Revolution*. Cambridge, MA: Harvard University Press, 2004.

———. *Haiti: The Aftershocks of History*. New York: Metropolitan Books, 2012.

Dudley, Will. *Hegel and History*. Albany: State University of New York Press, 2009.

Edmonds, Ennis B., and Michelle A. Gonzalez. *Caribbean Religious History: An Introduction*. New York: New York University Press, 2010.

Erskine, Noel Leo. *Plantation Church: How African American Religion was Born in Caribbean Slavery*. Oxford: Oxford University Press, 2014.

Fackenheim, Emil. *The Religious Dimension in Hegel's Thought*. Bloomington: Indiana University Press, 1968.

Fils-Aimé, Jean. *Vodou, je me souviens: le combat d'une culture pour sa survie*. Montreal: Éditions Dabar, 2007.

Flikschuh, Katrin. *Kant and Modern Political Philosophy*. Cambridge: Cambridge University Press, 2004.

Formosa, Paul. *Kantian Ethics, Dignity and Perfection*. Cambridge: Cambridge University Press, 2017.

Frère, Gérard A. "Haitian Voodoo: Its True Face". *Caribbean Quarterly* 24, nos. 3–4 (1978): 37–47.

Frierson, Patrick R. *Freedom and Anthropology in Kant's Moral Philosophy*. Cambridge: Cambridge University Press, 2003.

Gates, Brian Edwards. *Afro-Caribbean Religions*. London: Ward Lock Educational, 1980.

Gibson, Carrie. *Empire's Crossroads: A History of the Caribbean from Columbus to the Present Day*. New York: Atlantic Monthly Press, 2014.

Gibson, Kean. *Comfa Religion and Creole Language in a Caribbean Community*. Albany: State University of New York Press, 2001.

Guyer, Paul, ed. *The Cambridge Companion to Kant and Modern Philosophy.* Cambridge: Cambridge University Press, 2006.

———. *Kant on Freedom, Law, and Happiness.* Cambridge: Cambridge University Press, 2000.

Hanna, Robert. *Kant, Science and Human Nature.* Oxford: Oxford University Press, 2006.

Hegel, G.W.F. *Early Theological Writings.* Translated by T.M. Knox. Philadelphia: University of Pennsylvania Press, 1971.

———. *Lectures on the Philosophy of Religion*, vol. 2. Edited by Peter Hodgson; translated by R.F. Brown, P.C. Hodgson and J.M. Stewart. Berkeley: University of California Press, 1987.

———. *Phenomenology of Spirit.* Translated by A.V. Miller. Oxford: Oxford University Press, 1977.

———. *The Philosophy of History.* Translated by J. Sibree. New York: Prometheus Books, 1991.

———. *Philosophy of Mind.* Translated by A.V. Miller. Oxford: Oxford University Press, 1971.

———. *The Science of Logic.* Translated by George Di Giovanni. Cambridge: Cambridge University Press, 2010.

Henke, Holger, and Karl-Heinz Magister, eds. *Constructing Vernacular Culture in the Trans-Caribbean.* Lanham, MD: Lexington, 2008.

Henrich, Dieter. *Aesthetic Judgment and the Moral Image of the World: Studies in Kant.* Stanford: Stanford University Press, 1994.

Hodgson, Peter C., ed. *G.W.F. Hegel: Theologian of the Spirit.* Edinburgh: Augsburg Fortress, 1997.

Hoffe, Otfried. *Immanuel Kant.* Translated by Marshal Farrier. Albany: State University of New York Press, 1994.

Huneman, Phillippe. Ed. *Understanding Purpose: Kant and the Philosophy of Biology.* Rochester, NY: University of Rochester Press, 2007.

Hurston, Zora Neale. *Tell My Horse: Voodoo and Life in Haiti and Jamaica.* New York: Harpers and Row, 1990.

Huxley, Francis. *The Invisibles: Voodoo Gods in Haiti.* New York City: McGraw-Hill, 1966.

Inwood, Michael. *A Commentary on Hegel's Philosophy of Mind.* Oxford: Oxford University Press, 2010.

James, C.L.R. *The Black Jacobins: Toussaint L'Ouverture and the San Domingo Revolution.* New York: Vintage, 1989.

Jean, Joseph Jean. *God in the Haitian Voodoo Religion.* Pittsburgh: Dorrance, 2004.

Kant, Immanuel. *Anthropology from a Pragmatic Point of View*. Cambridge: Cambridge University Press, 2006.

——. *Anthropology, History, and Education*. Edited by Gunter Zoller and Robert B. Louden; translated by Mary Gregor, Paul Guyer, Gunter Zoller, Holly Wilson, Robert B. Louden, Allen W. Wood and Arnulf Zweig. Cambridge: Cambridge University Press, 2007.

——. *Critique of Practical Reason*. Translated by Mary Gregor. Cambridge: Cambridge University Press, 1997.

——. *Groundwork of the Metaphysics of Morals*. Translated by Lewis White Beck as *Foundations of the Metaphysics of Morals*. Trenton, NJ: Library of Liberal Arts, 1959.

——. *Lectures on Anthropology*. Edited by Allen W. Wood and Robert B. Louden; translated by Robert R. Clewis, Robert B. Louden, G. Felicitas Munzel and Allen W. Wood. Cambridge: Cambridge University Press, 2012.

——. *The Science of Right*. New York: Simon and Schuster, 2012.

——. *What Is Enlightenment?* Translated by Lewis White Beck. Trenton, NJ: Library of Liberal Arts, 1997.

Kaufmann, Walter. *Debating the Political Philosophy of Hegel*. New Brunswick, NJ: Transaction Books, 1970.

Kolb, David, ed. *New Perspectives on Hegel's Philosophy of Religion*. Albany: State University of New York Press, 1992.

Korner, Stephan. *Kant*. New York: Penguin, 1990.

Korsgaard, Christine. *Creating the Kingdom of Ends*. Cambridge: Cambridge University Press, 1996.

Kremser, Manfred. *African Caribbean Religions*. Vienna: Webster University Vienna, 1994.

Labuschagne, Bart, and Timo Slootweg, eds. *Hegel's Philosophy of the Historical Religions*. Leiden, Netherlands: Koninklijke Brill, 2012.

Laguerre, Michel S. *Voodoo and Politics in Haiti*. New York: St Martin's Press, 1989.

Lampe, Armando, ed. *Christianity in the Caribbean: Essays in Church History*. Kingston: University of the West Indies Press, 2001.

Lemoine, Maurice. *Bitter Sugar: Slaves Today in the Caribbean*. Chicago: Banner Press, 1985.

Lum, Kenneth Anthony. *Praising His Name in the Dance: Spirit Possession in the Spiritual Baptist Faith and Orisha Work in Trinidad, West Indies*. Australia: Hardwood Academic, 2000.

Magnus, Kathlee Dow. *Hegel and the Symbolic Mediation of Spirit*. Albany: State University of New York Press, 2001.

Maker, William, ed. *Hegel and Aesthetics: An Anthology of Experience*. Albany: State University of New York Press, 2000.
Martin, Gottfried. *Kant's Metaphysics and Theory of Science*. Translated by P.G. Lucas. Manchester: Manchester University Press, 1955.
Mazama, Ama. "Lwa". In *The Encyclopedia of African Religion*, vol. 1, edited by Molefi Kete Asante and Ama Mazama, 390–400. Los Angeles: Sage, 2009.
McCarney, Joseph. *Routledge Philosophy Guidebook to Hegel on History*. New York: Routledge, 2000.
Michel, Claudine, and Patrick Bellegarde-Smith, eds. *Vodou in Haitian Life and Culture: Invisible Powers*. New York: Palgrave Macmillan, 2006.
Mills, Patricia Jagentowicz, ed. *Feminist Interpretations of Hegel*. University Park: Pennsylvania State University Press, 1996.
Mitchell, Mozella. *Crucial Issues in Caribbean Religion*. New York: Peter Lang, 2006.
Montilus, Guérin. "Haïti: un cas témoin de la vivacité des religions africaines en Amérique et pourquoi". In *Vodun*. Paris: Présence Africaine, 1993.
Moyar, Dean, ed. *The Oxford Handbook of Hegel*. Cambridge: Cambridge University Press, 2017.
Murrell, Nathaniel S. *Caribbean Religions: An Introduction to Their Historical, Cultural and Sacred Traditions*. Philadelphia: Temple University Press, 2010.
Nancy, Jean-Luc. *Hegel: The Restlessness of the Negative*. Translated by Jason Smith and Steven Miller. Minneapolis: University of Minnesota Press, 2002.
Nesbitt, Nick. *Universal Emancipation: The Haitian Revolution and the Radical Enlightenment*. Charlottesville: University of Virginia Press, 2008.
Nicholls, David. *From Dessalines to Duvalier: Race, Colour and National Independence in Haiti*. New Brunswick, NJ: Rutgers University Press, 1996.
Nuzzo, Angelica, ed. *Hegel and the Analytic Tradition*. London: Continuum, 2011.
———. *Memory, History, Justice in Hegel*. London: Palgrave Macmillan, 2012.
O'Brien, George. *Hegel on Reason and History: A Contemporary Interpretation*. Chicago: University of Chicago Press, 1975.
Olmos, Margarite, and Lizabeth Paravisini-Gebert, eds. *Creole Religions of the Caribbean: An Introduction from Vodou and Santeria to Obeah and Espiritsimo*. New York: New York University Press, 2011.
———. *Sacred Possessions: Vodou, Santeria, Obeah, and the Caribbean*. New Brunswick, NJ: Rutgers University Press, 1997.
Olupona, Jacob K., and Terry Rey, eds. *Orisa Devotion as World Religion: The Globalization of Yoruba Religious Culture*. Madison: University of Wisconsin Press, 2008.

Ott, Thomas. *The Haitian Revolution.* Knoxville: University of Tennessee Press, 1973.
Paolucci, Anne A., and Henry Paolucci. *Hegel on Tragedy.* Westport, CT: Greenwood, 1975.
Patton, H.J. *The Categorical Imperative: A Study in Kant's Moral Philosophy.* Philadelphia: University of Pennsylvania Press, 1947.
Payne, Charlon, and Lucas Thorpe, eds. *Kant and the Concept of Community.* Rochester, NY: University of Rochester Press, 2011.
Pinn, Anthony. *Varieties of African-American Religious Experience.* Minneapolis: Augsburg Fortress Press, 1998.
Pinkard, Terry. *Does History Make Sense?: Hegel on the Historical Shapes of Justice.* Cambridge: Cambridge University Press, 2017.
Pulis, J.W., ed. *Religion, Diaspora, and Cultural Identity: A Reader in the Anglophone Caribbean.* Philadelphia: Gordon and Breach, 1999.
Renda, Mary A. *Taking Haiti: Military Occupation and the Culture of U.S. Imperialism, 1915–1940.* Chapel Hill: University of North Carolina Press, 2001.
Roberts, Neil. *Freedom as Maronnage.* Chicago: University of Chicago Press, 2015.
Rockmore, Tom. *Before and after Hegel: A Historical Introduction to Hegel's Thought.* Berkeley: University of California Press, 1993.
———. *Kant and Idealism.* New Haven: Yale University Press, 2007.
Rolph-Trouillot, Michel. "An Unthinkable History: The Haitian Revolution as a Non-Event". In *Haitian History: New Perspectives*, edited by Alyssa Sepinwall, 33–54. London: Routledge, 2013.
Rose, Gillian. *Hegel Contra Sociology.* London: Verso, 2009.
Rosen, Allen D. *Kant's Theory of Justice.* Ithaca: Cornell University Press, 1994.
Russon, John Edward. *Reading Hegel's Phenomenology.* Bloomington: Indiana University Press, 2004.
Sassen, Brigitte, ed. *Kant's Early Critics: The Empiricist Critique of the Theoretical Philosophy.* Translated by Brigitte Sassen. Cambridge: Cambridge University Press, 2000.
Saunders, Nicholas J. *The Peoples of the Caribbean: An Encyclopedia of Archeology and Traditional Culture.* Santa Barbara, CA: ABC-Clio, 2005.
Schmidt, Bettina E. *Caribbean Diaspora in the USA: Diversity of Caribbean Religions in New York City.* Burlington, VT: Ashgate, 2008.
Sensen, Oliver. *Kant on Human Dignity.* Berlin: Walter DeGruyter, 2011.
Shell, Susan Meld. *Kant and the Limits of Autonomy.* Cambridge, MA: Harvard University Press, 2009.

Sher, Philip W., ed. *Perspectives on the Caribbean: A Reader in Culture, History, and Representation*. Hoboken: Wiley-Blackwell, 2010.

Simpson, George E. *Black Religions in the New World*. New York: Columbia University Press, 1978.

Singh, Aakash, and Rimina Mohapatra, ed. *Reading Hegel: The Introductions*. Victoria: Re-Press, 2008.

Sjørslev, Inger. "Possession and Syncretism: Spirits as Mediators in Modernity". In *Reinventing Religions: Syncretism and Transformation in Africa and the Americas*, edited by Sidney M. Greenfield and André Droogers, 21–42. Lanham, MD: Rowman and Littlefield, 2001.

Smith, Matthew J. *Red and Black in Haiti: Radicalism, Conflict, and Political Change, 1934–1957*. Chapel Hill: University of North Carolina Press, 2009.

Somers-Hall, Henry. *Hegel, Deleuze, and the Critique of Representation: Dialectics of Negation and Difference*. Albany: State University of New York Press, 2012.

Stern, Robert. *Hegel, Kant and the Structure of the Object*. New York: Routledge, 1996.

Stratton-Lake, Philip. *Kant, Duty, and Moral Duty*. New York: Routledge, 2000.

Taylor, Charles. *Hegel*. Cambridge: Cambridge University Press, 1975.

Taylor, Patrick, ed. *Nation Dance: Religion, Identity, and Cultural Difference in the Caribbean Thought*. Bloomington: Indiana University Press, 2001.

Teo, Thomas. *The Critique of Psychology: From Kant to Postcolonial Theory*. New York: Springer, 2005.

Thomson, Garrett. *On Kant*. Belmont: Wadsworth, 2003.

Trost, Theodore Louis, ed. *The African Diaspora and the Study of Religion*. New York: Palgrave Macmillan, 2007.

Warner-Lewis, Maureen. *Central Africa in the Caribbean: Transcending Time, Transforming Cultures*. Kingston: University of the West Indies Press, 2003.

Wike, Victoria S. *Kant on Happiness in Ethics*. Albany: State University of New York Press, 1994.

Wilkins, Burleigh. *Hegel's Philosophy of History*. Ithaca: Cornell University Press, 1974.

Williams, Howard Loyd. *Essays on Kant's Political Philosophy*. Chicago: University of Chicago Press, 1992.

Williams, Robert R. *Recognition: Hegel and Fichte on the Other*. Albany: State University of New York Press, 1992.

Williamson, Raymond Keith. *An Introduction to Hegel's Philosophy of Religion*. Albany: State University of New York Press, 1984.

Wood, Allen W. *Kant's Ethical Thought*. Cambridge: Cambridge University Press, 1999.

Zammito, John H. *The Genesis of Kant's Critique of Pure Judgment*. Chicago: University of Chicago Press, 1992.

———. *Kant, Herder and the Birth of Anthropology*. Chicago: University of Chicago Press, 2002.

Zane, Wallace. *Journeys to the Spiritual Lands: The Natural History of a West Indian Religion*. Oxford: Oxford University Press, 1999.

Index

African Diaspora Enlightenment, 5
African cultures: culture traits
  and Haitian subjectivity, 9–10;
  misrepresentation by Hegel, 42–43, 45,
  46–51; synthesis of in Vodou, 9, 33–34,
  36, 39
African languages and Creole, 68
Alcide, Marie-José, 14
Arada. *See* Rada
Atlantic Cosmologies, 53–54

bagi (alter room), 11
Bondye, 22
Boukman Dutty (Zamba), 68–69
Brandom, Robert B., 32
Buck-Morss, Susan, 2, 42–43; conflation
  of Vodou and Freemasonry, 52–54;
  misrepresentation of Haitian
  Revolution, 54–57

Catholicism and syncretism, 12, 13,
  20–22
cemeteries, 15
Christian symbols in Vodou, 11–12
collective consciousness, 37
collective experience: and farming, 18;
  of forced labour and slavery, 2, 36–37;
  and subjectivity, 7; through theolepsy,
  40–41; of Vodou rituals, 11–12, 20, 36
Creole (Haitian), 68–69
creolization, as expressed through
  Vodou, 13, 21–22
cultural memory, 12

Davis, Wade, 35
deities in Vodou, 18, 22–23. *See also* Rada
  and Petro
Deren, Maya, 9
Desquiron, Lilas, 10, 12–13, 65
Dorsainvil, Justin, 8
Dubois, Laurent, 15

Enlightenment (Western), 26, 59–60;
  Vodou cosmology situated in, 7, 16,
  40–41; critique of, 58–59, 61–64
Enlightenment (radical), Haitian
  Revolution as, 70
ethical experience in Vodou cosmology,
  37–38, 38–40

Fils-Aimé, Jean, 23–24
forced labour: collective experience of, 2,
  3, 7, 25–26, 37; and self-consciousness,
  16–18; and Enlightenment ideals, 5, 59,
  70. *See also* slavery
freedom of will, 25; Kant and, 27–32;
  collective nature in Vodou, 32
Freemasonry, 43, 52–54

Genius compared to lwas, 52

Haitian Creole, 68–69
Haitian folklore, 8
Haitian Revolution: importance of
  Vodou for, 36–37, 58–59, 69–71;
  Maroons and, 69–70; misrecognition
  by Buck-Morss, 54; misrecognition by

89

Hegel, 54–57; omission by Hegel, 43

Haitian Vodou: academic interpretations of, 8; contemporary practice of, 17–18; deities of, 18–20; provenance of, 9, 13. *See also* Vodou; Vodou cosmology

Hegel, G.W.F., 1–2; and Christianity, 46, 57; formative activity, 16; Genius and lwas, 52; Haitian subjectivity, 7; misrecognition of the Haitian Revolution, 54–57; omission of Haitian Revolution, 2–3, 42–43; *Philosophy of History* lectures, 46, 55; *Philosophy of Mind* lectures, 56; Protestant biases, 3, 42–46; rationalization of slavery, 42; universal history, 43–44, 46; view of Africans, 3–4, 5, 42, 45, 46–51

hounfor (Vodou temple), public rituals of the, 11

houngan (Voodoo priest), 12

hounsis (Voodoo initiates), 12

Hurston, Zora Neale, 22

James, C.L.R., 17, 36

Kant, Immanuel, 1–2; concept of freedom of will, 28, 30–31, 32; concept of obligation, 29–30; concept of reasonableness, 26–28, 31–32; concept of universality, 28–31; good and evil compared with lwas modalities, 38; view of Africans, 48; view of slavery, 58–59, 60–61

Korsgaard, Christine, 28

Le Code Noir, 5, 13, 14, 21, 54, 66, 67, 70

Lemoine, Maurice, 34

loas (mystères), 22. *See also* lwas (spirits)

Lord and Bondsman, 7, 16

lwas (spirits): and freedom of will, 34–37; function of, 18, 23–24

Marinette-Bois-Cheche (Marinette-Dry-Bones), 24

Marronage: definition of, 4; and freedom, 58, 67–69; and social agency, 70

monarchy, tyranny of the, 5, 60–61, 70

moral autonomy, issue of, 25–26

Négritude movement, 8

Neo-African cults, 12

Nesbitt, Nick, 70

Nicholls, David, 11

obligation, concept of; in Kant, 29–30; and collective consciousness in Vodou, 37

Petro (lwas), 18–20, 22, 23; as unreasonable modality, 37–38

Phenomenology of Spirit, (Hegel), 7, 42

Philosophy of Mind (Hegel), 42

Pinkard, Terry, 55

Pinn, Anthony, 19

Price-Mars, Jean, 8

Rada (lwas), 18, 22, 23; as reasonable modality, 37–38

rituals: and African ancestors, 9–11; within the lakou, 15; lwas in, 18–20; social bonding and collective identity, 14–17; in Vodun, 51–52. *See also* sub-Saharan African religious practices; Vodou, rituals

Roberts, Neil, 4, 58

Rolph-Trouillot, Michel, 5, 59, 61–64, 68–69

Rose, Gillian, 17

Saint-Domingue; collective experience of slaves on, 7, 65–71
The Science of Right (Kant), 60
slavery: view of by Kant and Hegel, 60–62; and subjectivity, 67–68
slave trade (Atlantic), 52–53
Spirit, 46–47, 57
spirit possession. *See* theolepsy
subjectivity: Haitian collective self[consciousness, 16, 17, 18, 40–41, 66; Haitian compared to Western form of, 13, 26, 33, 66; Haitian form of, 7, 9–10, 67
sub-Saharan African religious practices: Hegel's misunderstanding of, 46–51; and Vodun, 51–52. *See also* rituals; West African beliefs and practices; Vodou, rituals
syncretism, paradigm of, 9–10, 12

theolepsy (spirit possession), 38–39; and collective experience, 40–41
transatlantic slave trade, 42, 52–53

universal history: of Kant, 46; as interpreted by Buck-Morss, 54
Universality, 28–29, 43–46

vévés (symbolic signs of the gods), 12
Vodun, 51–52
Vodou: and Catholic saints, 22; ceremonies, 12, 19; clash between clergy and practitioners of, 21; collective nature of, 36; conflation with Freemasonry, 52–57; and religious syncretism, 21, 53; restoring of family structure, 11; rituals, 64–67; secular dimension of, 7–8
Vodou cosmology: and Atlantic Cosmologies, 53–54; collective identity in, 14–17; contextualized within the Enlightenment, 16, 26; definition of, 1, 7–8; ethical experience in, 37–38, 38–40; freedom of will in, 32–37; and geography, 18, 67–68; physical layout of, 11; as requisite for Haitian nation-building, 58–59, 64–68, 70; syncretic nature of, 9–10, 65–66

What Is Enlightenment? (Kant), 59
West African beliefs and practices, 11. *See also* sub-Saharan African religious practices

www.ingramcontent.com/pod-product-compliance
Lightning Source LLC
Chambersburg PA
CBHW031637160426

43196CB00006B/455